Praise for Linda Wolfe's

Wasted
Inside the Robert Chambers–Jennifer Levin Murder
A *New York Times* "Notable Book of the Year"

"Breadth, subtlety . . . fierce intelligence. Wolfe . . . ended up knowing more about Jennifer Levin than her father did and more about Robert Chambers than his mother wanted to."

—John Leonard, *New York* magazine

"A real-life incident ordained as an American tragedy."

—*Los Angeles Times Book Review*

"A compelling, seamless read."

—*The Plain Dealer* (Cleveland)

"A real page-turner . . . A thoughtful and unsensational book about a thoughtless and horrifying murder."

—*Mademoiselle*

Double Life
The Shattering Affair between Chief Judge Sol Wachtler and Socialite Joy Silverman

"[A] shocking Jekyll-and-Hyde tale."

—Maureen Dowd, *The New York Times Book Review*

"Linda Wolfe has written yet another spellbinding tale. . . . *Double Life* is such an intimate portrait that I felt like a voyeur—but could not stop until I finished the last page."

—Ann Rule, *New York Times* bestselling
author of *Bitter Harvest*

Also by Linda Wolfe

Double Life
Wasted
The Professor and the Prostitute
Playing Around
Private Practices (a novel)
The Literary Gourmet

LOVE ME TO DEATH

LINDA WOLFE

POCKET BOOKS

New York London Toronto Sydney Tokyo Singapore

POCKET BOOKS, a division of Simon & Schuster Inc.
1230 Avenue of the Americas, New York, NY 10020

Copyright © 1998 by Gayle Hallenbeck Lynds

Originally published in hardcover in 1998 by Pocket Books

ISBN: 0-671-51732-5

First Pocket Books paperback printing November 1999

10   9   8   7   6   5   4   3   2   1

POCKET and colophon are registered trademarks of
Simon & Schuster Inc.

Front cover credits: couple dancing © Aldo Sessa; Richard
Caputo courtesy of San Francisco Police Department

Printed in the U.S.A.

QB/✖

For M.P.

The manifold labyrinth my steps
wove through all these years since childhood
has brought me to this ruinous afternoon.

—Jorge Luis Borges
"Conjectural Poem"

ACKNOWLEDGMENTS

Many of the people who helped me to write this book are mentioned in the text, but I'd like to single out Earl Sanders, assistant chief of police in San Francisco, California; John McGrath, a private investigator on Long Island, New York; Elise McCarthy, assistant district attorney of Nassau County, New York; and Clem Patti, assistant district attorney of Westchester County, New York. Their encouragement and assistance were invaluable. Not mentioned in the text, but also of great assistance, were Maj. Louis Souza of the Honolulu, Hawaii, police department and Immigration inspector Miguel Guerrero, of the El Paso Detention Facility in Texas.

I am also deeply indebted to my editors at Pocket Books: to Bill Grose, who first suggested that I try to tell this tale and whose vision of how it might best be told challenged me to stretch myself as a writer; and to Emily Bestler, who inherited the manuscript upon his retirement but treated it not as a foundling but as her very own scion.

Additionally, I'd like to thank Jessica Bernstein, who read the manuscript and provided sensitive and useful suggestions, and Alan Friedman, Daniel

Pollack-Pelzner, Deborah Pollack, three other readers who were helpful in spotting rough spots.

I owe special thanks to Dr. Helen Singer Kaplan, who died before I completed the book but who even while ill was generous in offering emotional support and astute psychological insights. I am grateful, too, to Dr. Ethel Person, again for psychological insights, and also for helping me gain entry into the world of Argentinian psychiatry, and to Malcolm Taub, who shared with me his considerable knowledge of Argentina.

I also appreciate Martha Blumberg and Lourdes Bautista, for their help in translating, respectively, the Spanish poetry and documents used in the text; Michael Kelly, for transcribing lengthy interviews; and Naomi Bernstein, surely the best researcher any writer could hope to find.

But to none of these people do I owe the thanks due my husband. I'd have floundered indeed without his sagacity, patience, and care during the three years this book was in the making.

Author's Note

The information in this book comes from the interviews I conducted with scores of people involved with Ricardo Caputo or his victims, as well as from police and court documents and newspaper articles. The narrative accounts of what transpired between Caputo and individuals now dead, including material in direct quotation, are drawn from the investigations conducted by the police with associates of the dead individuals, except in one or two instances where, because no other information was available, I made use of information tendered to me by Caputo that I judged to be true.

All the names used in the book are actual, except for those of the woman Caputo attempted to rape in 1975, the woman who kept a diary about him in 1982 and 1983, and the woman who had an affair with him in Mexico City in 1977, who are referred to here as Mary O'Neill, Lotte Angstrom, and Maria Lopez, respectively.

for that good life had ended for him once he ca
to the United States, or so he said. Here, he'd

PROLOGUE

Not long ago a man who had been on the run for twenty years, altering his appearance, buying new birth certificates, commandeering new social security numbers, moving from one impersonal American city to another, and slipping back and forth across the country's easy borders, confessed to having murdered several women with whom he'd had lengthy love affairs and voluntarily turned himself in for the killings. The women had all been attractive, accomplished, intelligent—one had worked for a bank, another had been a psychologist, another a film editor, another a graduate student at a university. They'd met the murderer through their work or while relaxing at cafés or bars, and he'd pleased them with his handsome looks, friendly smile, and artistic talent, as well as with the amusing stories he told about the good life he'd led as a boy in Latin America. They'd also felt sorry for him, for that good life had ended for him once he came to the United States, or so he said. Here, he'd become just another Latino, a victim of prejudice and restrictive visas, who'd had to hide from immigration authorities and take low-visibility and low-end jobs, work that was far beneath his abilities.

The women were touched by his travails and enthralled by his charms. They dated him, took him home and to bed with them, introduced him to their friends and their parents, and had no idea that what lay in store for them when they decided to end their relationship with him was a knife in the chest, a nylon stocking tied around the throat, a brutal and fatal beating.

The murderer went by many names during his years on the lam, seventeen names in all. But his real name was Ricardo Caputo.

PART ONE
THE WOMEN

1

I remember clearly the day—it was over a dozen years ago—that I first heard the name Ricardo Caputo. The person who mentioned the name to me was a private detective who'd been hired to find out who had murdered a New York writer, a woman noted for philanthropy and social activism. The detective had been on the case for a year and a half, and on a February afternoon in 1985 he informed me that he at last knew the killer. It was Caputo.

I remember how relieved I was to hear the name. It didn't mean anything to me—any name would have done. And the feeling of relief didn't last long. In a few minutes, it would dissipate, then vanish altogether. But before I get to that, let me explain why I was at least momentarily relieved. It was because I'd known and admired Jacqui Bernard, the dead woman, and had long been hoping that the mystery of her death would be solved.

I'd even tried to solve it myself. Amateur sleuth that I was, after Jacqui was killed in the summer of 1983, I spent weeks interviewing people who might be able to shed light on her murder and published my findings, such as they were, in an article in *New York* magazine. At the time, I was relatively new to crime reporting. I was also shy, not the kind of person to whom asking questions of strangers came easily. Still, I managed to turn out a fairly decent piece of work about Jacqui, and because of this I'd gotten to know McEwan. He'd looked me up after my article appeared and we'd become friends of a sort. Phone pals, mostly, though occasionally we got together for a talk, a meal.

I enjoyed knowing him. Writing about Jacqui, I'd become obsessed with discovering who had killed her, and McEwan shared that obsession. Our reasons were different. He was on a job. I was just intensely curious. I think it was because Jacqui's murder had spoken to a particular fear of mine—and, I believe, of many women. She'd been killed not by a stranger but by someone she knew, someone who hadn't had to sneak into her home or force his way into her room. She had let her killer in. Or come home with him. She had been killed by an intimate.

I hadn't known this at first, and neither had the police. Indeed, at first they hadn't even believed that Jacqui had been murdered. Her body had been found by her sister and brother-in-law, who'd been expecting her for dinner. When she failed to show up, they went to her apartment to see if anything was wrong. They got a key from a member of the co-op board, let themselves in, and saw Jacqui lying facedown on her bed, her head leaning against a small velvet pillow. She didn't stir, and they realized she was dead.

Nothing suggested foul play. When the police arrived at the spacious co-op, they observed that it hadn't been broken into—not just the door but all the window locks were still intact. They noted, too, that the rooms showed no signs of disarray. No drawers had been dumped, no closets ransacked, and the bed on which the dead woman lay wasn't rumpled or disturbed. The only odd thing was that she was wearing a long-sleeved bathrobe—odd because it was an exceedingly hot night and her apartment had no air-conditioning. But strokes and cardiac arrests weren't altogether uncommon in women of Jacqui's age, which was sixty-two. Maybe, the police reasoned, she'd put on the robe because a sudden chill had presaged an incipient heart attack or stroke.

This view was shared by the medical examiner the police summoned to look over the body. The ME pronounced that Jacqui had died of natural causes.

But of what sort of natural cause? Jacqui's sister wanted to know if she'd been sick or had a coronary, and she asked to have an autopsy performed. The body was taken to the medical examiner's office, and one of the doctors there undertook the slow, careful examination of every inch of flesh and expanse of inner organ. Not long after this second medical examiner began his autopsy, he noticed something the original ME had not. Jacqui's larynx had been fractured. She had been strangled to death by someone with strong, deadly fingers.

It was at this point that Gordon McEwan had entered the picture. Having lost confidence in the police, Jacqui's sister had enlisted him to look into what had happened to her. He and his partner had gone to her apartment, searched the rooms, and found something, a clue—a yellow towel or bed-spread, a close friend of Jacqui's told me—though exactly what the clue was and what its significance might be, I certainly didn't know. Not when I wrote my article. At that time, given that the cause of her death was a mystery and few facts about it were at my disposal, I wrote as much about Jacqui's life as about her death.

It had been a remarkable life. Although Jacqui's father was a French count, she'd been raised in America, where she had grown up to eschew the aristocratic and champion the rights of the disconsolate and disadvantaged. She'd cofounded the famous organization Parents Without Partners. She'd raised money for the historic black-voter-registration drive in Mississippi. She'd taught remedial reading and writing at a college designed to educate minority students. She'd done volunteer work for an association devoted to stopping human rights violations. She'd started a foundation to help illiterate Southern women record their oral histories, using her own money to fund the grants. And she'd published two well-received works of nonfiction, *Voices From the Southwest,* a collection of profiles of Native Americans, and *Journey Toward Freedom,* a biography of the black abolitionist and early feminist Sojourner Truth.

In the period before her death, Jacqui's interests had shifted toward Hispanic politics and culture. Just before her murder, she had joined an organization that supported the left-wing regime in Nicaragua and had spent two weeks in Cuba at a health conference.

Jacqui's passion for social action was paralleled by a tireless devotion to her friends. The divorced mother of one child, a son, Jacqui had never remarried, but instead she'd surrounded herself with friends, men and women alike, lavishing on them a maternal and inspirational affection. She'd had scores of friends, but she'd always been open to meeting just one more.

When I wrote my article about Jacqui, I interviewed people who'd known her far better and far longer than I had. A few of them feared, they told me, that her political activities might have had something to do with her death. But most were convinced that the motive for her killing was robbery: once her apartment was thoroughly searched, her purse and a gold watch were found to be missing.

One of Jacqui's best friends had a theory about who might have stolen these items and then killed Jacqui—but no name to attach to her theory. She informed me that Jacqui had recently mentioned she'd been dating a man she'd met in a local bar, a fellow who had thoroughly charmed her. "I think *he* killed her," her friend said. "It was probably just like in that book, *Mr. Goodbar*."

I still have the notes I took of that conversation: "She met a guy in the West End Cafe about six months ago. A young guy. Black or Hispanic. She said he was very attracted to her." And I can still remember thinking as I scribbled that Jacqui must have felt proud about garnering such a fellow's attentions, for although she *was* attractive, she was no longer young, no longer at an age when a woman hears with some regularity that this man or that finds her appealing. I expressed this thought to the woman who told me about the man in the West End Cafe, and she replied, prophetically it would turn out, "I keep wondering what sort of guy this fellow was. The kind of younger guy who really digs older women? Or just a con artist feeding her a line."

I was fascinated by this particular friend's information, though it was just a tidbit leading to an insight that went nowhere. Still, I kept thinking about it even after my article appeared, and I kept mulling over the other clues I'd gotten. Such as the long-sleeved robe. Why had she been wearing that on such a scorching night? And what about that yellow bedspread or towel? That *had* to be significant.

Because when I'd mentioned it to the police, they'd refused to comment about it.

But no matter how I tried to arrange and rearrange the pieces of the puzzle, it was all to no avail. Jacqui's fate continued to elude me, and I continued to be obsessed with it.

And then Gordon McEwan called. He asked me if I'd heard anything more about Jacqui's killer since my article came out, and I said, no, I hadn't. "Well, you never know," he said. "You might. You journalists hear things."

I was flattered by his perception of me as a skilled investigator who might yet produce important leads, and when he added that he'd like us to get to know each other, just in case one day I did hear something that might prove useful, I cheerfully said I'd like that, too. Still, I thought he was talking in general terms, the equivalent of "Let's have lunch someday." But then he suggested, "Tomorrow?"

I speedily accepted. I'd never met a private eye before. Like most writers, despite the heady things I sometimes wrote about, I led a life that was essentially prosaic, populated by a husband and children and friends who did ordinary things—taught, counseled, labored at desks in busy offices. The idea of meeting a man who made his living by snooping intrigued me, partly because it seemed such an exotic way to earn one's livelihood and partly because, like all Americans, I'd grown up on books and movies about private eyes. Indeed I was sure, before I met McEwan the first time, that I knew just what to expect. I figured he'd be a rueful loner like Sam Spade, and that he'd speak in an oblique, tough American slang, like Philip Marlowe.

But McEwan wasn't like my collective vision of the private eye. For one thing, he was married and adored his wife and children, not to mention the huge collection of pets, of turtles and rabbits, snakes and ducks, he'd gathered for his family. For another, he was Scottish, and although, having been brought to the United States as a youngster, he did speak American slang, he spoke it with a lacing of the Queen's English and the hint of a lilting burr.

I liked him from the start. A well-built man who appeared to be in his mid-fifties, he was dressed in a suit and tie and had silvery hair, a taut-lipped smile, and sad, penetrating eyes that looked as if they'd seen many things their owner wished they hadn't. He was also sweet-natured, given to compliments. "I learned a lot about Jacqui from what you wrote," he said to me that first day. "You made her sound real special."

"She was," I said. "Feisty. Opinionated. But essentially a very giving person."

"Yeah. But of course, that was her undoing."

He launched then into a detective's view of personality. It was a view that took traits most of us think of as virtues and turned them around so that they came out as character flaws. I have since heard this view many times, from many other detectives, and have come to see some truth in it, but this was the first time, and it made me uneasy. "Your friend Jacqui was always befriending people. She was trusting. She was generous. She treated everybody equal. She acted the way religion and ethics tell us to. But you know, it really ain't smart. It gets you killed."

He was filled with other police theories that have since become familiar to me but which at the time were new and slightly perplexing. "Jacqui must have gotten herself involved with a psychopath," he said, "the kind of person—it could have been a man or a woman, but most likely it was a man—who's got no morality, no conscience. This one probably came on like a lost puppy. Told her he needed help, love."

How did he know? "Just a guess," he said. "A guess based on what we've found out about Jacqui. About her being bighearted."

He then went on to say something that sounded suspiciously like what is today called blaming the victim, and although I didn't know the phrase then, his words made me testy. "The psychopath chooses his victim," he said. "But the victim chooses him, too. Because she's got something in her that makes her willing."

"Willing to what?" I objected. "Bring about her own destruction?" I didn't believe, still don't, in that kind of ex post facto reasoning, though I'd heard it often enough from friends in thrall to inferior psychotherapists. But McEwan, as it turned out, didn't mean that Jacqui was self-destructive. "Take it easy," he said. "You're getting on the wrong trolley. I don't think your friend wanted to die. I'm just saying there's a kind of tango between victimizers and their victims. I'm just saying that in a lot of these cases, you find a man who wants someone he can take from, and a woman who wants someone she can give to. A nurturer. He picks her, but in a way, she's also choosing, fastening on to someone who fits her particular receptors."

Once I understood what he was saying, McEwan's explanation sounded right to me. Jacqui *had* been a nurturer. Her whole life had been about helping people she perceived as needy. "Got you," I said, and moved on to whether there were any suspects.

McEwan shook his head. "Nobody who panned out."

"What do you do next?"

"Sit back and wait."

Body taut, eyes sharp, he made it sound as if sitting back and waiting was an active, not a passive, endeavor, and I thought of asking him, wait for what? But I let the opportunity slip by, inquiring instead about the clue he'd found. I'd rehearsed that question from the moment we'd made our appointment. "Tell me what it was you found in Jacqui's apartment. The towel. Or was it a bedspread? The police would never tell me."

"The police?" he muttered disdainfully—though, as I would later find out, he'd been on the police force himself for more than twenty years before starting his investigative agency. "They wouldn't tell you because *they* didn't find it."

"What was it?"

"A bedspread. You want me to tell you about it?"

Something in his voice suggested that what he had to say was distressing, or at least that he wanted to be sure I could take being given the kind of information he was accustomed to imparting. I felt it so strongly that a part of me wanted to answer, no, forget it, but I knew I couldn't do that, not if I was ever going to succeed as a crime reporter. So I said, "Yes, what was so important about the bedspread?"

He told me. And afterward I was sorry, because I was never able to forget what he said or the picture it summoned up. "Me and my partner, John McGrath," he fired off, "went through Jacqui's place with a fine-tooth comb, opening all the closets and cupboards, looking at everything. And in a linen closet right next to the bed, we found this bedspread, a ribbed, light-colored spread, all rolled up. When we unrolled it, we saw it had feces on it. Jacqui's sister was in the other room, and I called out, 'Did Jacqui have a dog?' She said no. And we knew then what had happened. The killer had choked Jacqui and her bowels had let go, and he'd wiped her with the bedspread and dressed her in that long-sleeved, heavy robe she was found in."

I closed my eyes, but it didn't faze McEwan. He was too far into his story. Without any further prompting, he went on to explain why the bed-spread mattered. He said it showed that the killer had some fastidiousness, some shame about leaving his victim lying in excrement. "That's also why he didn't leave her naked, why he dressed her in the robe. It's usually a sign that the killer knew his vic-tim, had some sort of relationship with her."

Eyes open now, wide open, I burst out, "Could it have been the man she met in the West End Cafe?"

He shrugged. He'd heard that story, too. "Yeah. But who *is* that man? He could be anyone."

McEwan called me frequently over the next few months. "Heard anything?" he'd ask.

"No," I'd always say, and feel dejected. "How about you?"

But it was always no on his end, too. Still, he kept calling me. And one time he sent another private eye to talk to me, a detective named Frank Hickey, who was now working with him on the case. Hickey was young and redheaded, and he came to see me straight from the street, his hands specked with dirt, his jeans torn, his ancient T-shirt stained and ill-fit-ting. He looked like someone I'd give wide berth to if I ran into him on a West Side street corner. But for all his disguise, I didn't find Hickey threatening. He was funny and warm and proud of his sister, a TV newscaster. Besides, by this time I was getting used to private eyes, so fast does the exotic become old hat once you've had a little taste of it. I was also getting used to the monotony of being asked if I'd heard anything more about Jacqui's killer and the sadness of having to say I hadn't.

Hickey had posters with him that he'd put up all over my neighborhood, posters offering a $25,000 reward for information leading to the arrest and conviction of Jacqui's murderer. He left one with me, and for a long while after he departed, I stared at the photograph of Jacqui on the poster: Jacqui gray-haired, dignified, and smiling in that unusual way she had, a smile so ample that her cheeks got round and full and made one remember those drawings of the wind that decorate antique maps; Jacqui decked out in beaded hoop earrings and a turtleneck sweater that hugged her delicate throat. When I thought of her killer clutching that throat, then wiping and garbing her as if her body were his giant doll, I could scarcely keep from crying.

It was many months afterward that McEwan called me and said he knew who had killed Jacqui. "Who? Who?" I demanded. But he wouldn't tell me over the phone. "Let's get together," he said. "There's something I want to show you."

We made a date for drinks the next day. We met and sat down in a quiet Italian restaurant. And before we'd even ordered, he began talking. "The man who killed Jacqui," he said, "has killed other women. At least four more." McEwan was excited. "The sonovabitch!"

"How do you know?" I asked, impatient to learn the details.

"I got a call from an informant about three weeks ago. He said he'd gotten high with some Hispanic guy and the guy boasted that he'd killed Jacqui Bernard."

It was, I realized, just what McEwan had been hoping for when he'd said he'd just sit back and wait. I'd always imagined that killers buried the secret of their crimes deeper than gravediggers buried the bodies they left behind, but McEwan had known, as I hadn't then, that a vast number of killers get caught because they're proud of their savagery and sooner or later want to brag. "This guy's clever," McEwan went on. "But he's stupid, too. His name's Ricardo Caputo."

At this moment, I felt the relief I've mentioned earlier, at this moment and all the while that McEwan was telling me about his tipster. "My informant said he was calling in response to one of the posters Hickey and I put up," McEwan said. "Wouldn't give me his name. Said he'd been arrested in September 1983, gone to jail, got out a few months ago, and did drugs a few weeks ago with this Caputo fellow, who was living up around One Hundred and Fifty-eighth Street." McEwan's voice was breathless, as if he were running, not sitting on a banquette. "My informant had his girlfriend with him," he went on, "and she said something that made my fellow mad and Caputo said, 'Any bitch gives me trouble, I'd kill her.' Then the girlfriend left, and Caputo started bragging about how he really had killed people. Men as well as women. And he mentioned Jacqui Bernard specifically. Said he'd met her in a bar or at some sort of outing. Said she was too old for him but he started seeing her anyway. Because she was rich. Because she loaned him money. Let him use her car. Even said she'd help him out with a problem he was having with Immigration. She knew people who could fix it. Then one night, he went to her apartment to borrow her car. He needed it for some job. But this time, Jacqui didn't want him to have it—maybe she was starting to have her doubts about him. Anyway, she said no, and they started quarreling. And he strangled her."

"He killed her because she wouldn't lend him her *car*?" I said.

"He's probably killed for even less. He's been a busy sonovabitch. He killed a girl in Nassau County. Another one in Westchester. Two more after that." McEwan had gone to the New York police and to the FBI with his informant's story. They'd supplied him with a huge file on Caputo. "He stabbed and choked the first one. Strangled the next. The other two he beat to death. You want to know how?"

I had the same feeling I'd had when he'd asked if I wanted to know about the bedspread. But this time he didn't wait for my response. He just began talking, talking fast. Maybe he needed to get it off his chest. "One of them he stomped to death," he said. "The other one, he used an iron bar. And he tortured her first. Pulled out all her teeth."

I felt sick to my stomach. I *saw* those teeth. Little pearls encrusted with blood. But I was determined to play the role of an unflusterable journalist. It meant that out of sight and under the table, I clenched my hands together and that I swallowed hard, but as surreptitiously as I could. Then I got my voice back and I asked, "You sure it's the same guy?"

"Damn sure." He reached into the inside pocket of his jacket and pulled out a folded piece of paper. "This is what I wanted to show you."

It was a photograph—a copy of a photograph, to be exact. The picture showed a soulful-looking young man with deep-set eyes, a sensual cleft chin, a graceful bowed mouth, and wavy, windswept hair: a handsome, even beautiful, young man. "This is Caputo," McEwan said. "I got his picture from the FBI. And I've been showing it around. And you know what? I showed it to all the bartenders up near Jacqui's building, and one of them, the bartender at a place called Cannon's, said he'd seen this guy come into the bar. With Jacqui!" McEwan's voice was triumphant. "And that's not all. I showed it to the super at Jacqui's building. He recognized the face, too. He said that a short while after Jacqui was killed, he noticed this very guy trying to get into the building. He had some keys that didn't work, and when the super asked him what he wanted and who he was, the guy had a cock-and-bull story. 'I'm Jacqui Bernard's roommate,' he says, 'and I've got to get back into our apartment.' The super doesn't know anything about any roommate. Jacqui'd never mentioned one. So he says to the guy, 'Jacqui's dead, and the keys have been changed,' and the guy doesn't say a word, he just hurries away. But the super got a good look at him, and it was my guy. Caputo."

I was astonished. And happy, sure that the next thing McEwan would say was that Caputo was about to be taken into custody. "I guess that's it, then," I said, and smiled. "I guess you've found your man."

But McEwan didn't smile back. "I haven't *found* him," he muttered. "No one can find him. He's disappeared."

Disappeared? The word brought my nausea back full force. "Yeah," McEwan was saying. "He's still out there somewhere. And that's where you come in. I need a favor. I need you to get your magazine to run this picture."

I was still feeling sick, and I had a strong urge to put my hand over my mouth, but I swallowed again and nodded acquiescence.

"I *gotta* get the picture out there," McEwan said. "This guy could be anywhere. Here. Europe. South America. Who knows? But maybe someone'll see the picture and recognize him, tell us where he is."

The next day I called the editor who'd handled my story about Jacqui. I told him about Caputo and asked him to run the photograph. But the editor wasn't interested. "We can't run a photo of every guy

suspected of murder," he said to me. "What are we?
A post office wall?"

I wish I could say that I argued with him. But I
wasn't a bold person then. When my editor told me
no, I didn't put up a fight. I just subsided, reported
the conversation to McEwan, and told him unhappily that I couldn't help him.

That was pretty much the end of our dealings
with each other, although we continued to speak on
the phone for a few more months. Then I got busy
on a book that required my living in Boston for a
while, and McEwan got busy on other cases, and
after a time we drifted apart. But I was happy to see
when I turned on my television set one day in 1991
that he'd gotten Caputo's photograph "out there."
On the popular true-crime show *Unsolved Mysteries,*
there was McEwan, holding up the picture of
Caputo, recounting the story of how he'd shown it
around in Jacqui's neighborhood, and urging view-
ers to call the show if they knew the whereabouts of
the man in the picture.

Still, I gather that no one called. That is, no one
who really knew where Caputo was, though the show
got lots of tips and leads from people who said they'd
seen a man like the one in the picture, tips and leads
that the FBI checked out but that ultimately came to
nothing. Caputo was gone; dust gathered on the files
of the women the FBI had solid evidence he had
killed; and Jacqui's murder, for which he was now
viewed as the prime suspect, remained unsolved.

All of which is by way of explaining why, when I
unfolded my copy of the *New York Times* on the
morning of March 10, 1994, I was beside myself
with both amazement and excitement when I read,
right on the front page, that Ricardo Caputo, who
had been living in Mexico under an assumed name,
had fled that country for Argentina and had there

admitted who he was, confessed to having murdered several women, and arranged to turn himself in. He'd effectuated his surrender yesterday, the paper said, and was now in the custody of New York police. I wanted to share my amazement and excitement, and even though Jacqui's name wasn't among those Caputo had listed as his victims, and despite the fact that it was quite early in the morning, I reached for the phone and called McEwan.

A strange voice answered his phone. It was his old partner, John McGrath, a man I'd never met. "Gordon's gone," he said.

I thought he meant gone out, so I asked, "When can I reach him?"

"He's dead," McGrath said. "Died eighteen months ago. Cancer."

It was hard to believe, the way getting that sort of news about people with whom you've been out of touch is always hard to believe. You visualize them the way they were when you last saw them, and in McEwan's case the last time I'd seen him—nine years ago, I realized with a start—he'd been not just vigorous, but bursting with passion. Remembering his vitality on that day, I murmured, "I'm sorry. So very sorry."

"Me, too," McGrath sighed. "Especially today. Because Gordon would have been so happy today. The Caputo case drove him, you know."

"I do."

"It drove him almost to the day he died. He shoulda lived to see this."

"He should've."

"He shoulda got to meet that sonovabitch Caputo."

"So you think this Caputo really killed Jacqui Bernard?" I interrupted him, thinking as I did how much less reticent I'd become over the past decade,

how much the years I'd spent at crime reporting
since I'd first met McEwan had altered me, made
me come to inhabit the role I'd once merely practiced with him.

"Yeah. Probably," McEwan's old partner said.
"I've already talked to the police. They think he's
killed a lot more people than the ones whose murders he's admitted."

"Natalie Brown," I said, glancing down at my
newspaper. "Judith Becker. Barbara Taylor. Laura
Gomez."

"Yeah," McGrath snorted, "the ones we were
ninety-nine percent sure he killed. The ones he was
known to have been romancing."

They were all young women, much younger than
Jacqui had been. "Maybe he didn't want to admit he
romanced an older woman," I said.

"Yeah. Mr. Macho," McGrath snorted again.

After that, we spent a few moments talking about
why Caputo had turned himself in. The story we'd
both read in the paper made no sense. It was that
Caputo had suffered a sudden accession of remorse.
"You know, folks don't come down with remorse
like a flu or a head cold," McGrath said. "There's
gotta be more to the story." I agreed. But what was
the whole story? Neither of us could dope it out.
Then, "They're arraigning him this morning,"
McGrath said. "Out in Mineola."

As soon as he said that, I knew I was going to try
to write a book about Caputo. Partly it was because
I still imagined that I could solve the mystery of
Jacqui's death. But mostly it was because Caputo
had inhabited my mind for so many years that I
wanted to get him out of it, to exorcise him.

Mineola was half an hour by train from my
apartment. I said a hasty good-bye to McGrath and
headed for the railroad.

2

The Nassau County courtroom in which Caputo was about to be arraigned for the first killing to which he'd admitted—that of Natalie Brown—was jammed with TV and newspaper reporters by the time I got there, so jammed that I couldn't get a seat in the press rows up front. I slipped into a back pew, just in time to see Caputo, hands cuffed and legs chained, being led into the room by several court officers. This can't be him, I thought as he was unshackled. Not this paunchy, balding, glassy-eyed man. I couldn't put such an ill-favored apparition together with the man in the photograph McEwan had shown me, couldn't imagine him courting and seducing attractive and presumably discriminating women. But of course, I reminded myself, time and a life on the run would have taken their toll on the once comely young man.

Most of the press had already gotten their first glimpse of the forty-four-year-old Caputo. They'd been alerted the night before that there'd be an early "perp walk," the parading of a criminal as he leaves police headquarters and goes to his arraignment. I'd missed that stage-managed ritual. But, I comforted myself, at least I was seeing Caputo now, albeit from

a seat so far back that I could barely hear him when
in a whispered answer to a question of the presiding
judge, he allowed that he was represented by an
attorney.

Still, I heard the attorney, Park Avenue lawyer
Michael Kennedy, well enough. Kennedy, who numbered among his clients the glittering socialite Ivana
Trump, was a presence, a deep-voiced, confident
courtroom performer. I had met him once when
friends of mine took me with them to a benefit party
at his East Side condominium, a palatial duplex that,
with its sweeping staircase and grandly proportioned
living room, had reminded me of a ballroom.

It crossed my mind that Caputo must be a
wealthy man if he could afford to retain Kennedy.
Maybe during his years on the run, I thought, he
dealt drugs and secreted away a fortune. Either that
or someone in his family is wealthy and sufficiently
devoted to put up the money. His brother? In one of
his calls to me, McEwan had mentioned that
Ricardo had a brother named Alberto who'd
become a great success in America, opened a business of some sort. I made a note to try to find out
more about Alberto Caputo.

Then I got busy taking notes on what Kennedy
was saying, which was that before the case went forward, he wanted to be certain that his client was
given psychiatric medication to control his "terrible
schizophrenia." "He's had some medication pre-
scribed by an Argentinian doctor, but it will be
exhausted as of today," the lawyer intoned. "He
needs to receive immediate medical and psychiatric
attention."

The judge, a gentle-looking man who was wearing his black robe casually open at the neck, as if to
say he was no stickler for convention, granted the
request. He ordered tersely that Caputo be seen by

a prison psychiatrist as soon as possible, and moments later the arraignment was over.

Or rather, it was over for Caputo, who was led in his handcuffs and leg chains to the Nassau County jail. For Kennedy, there was still work to do, the work of affecting the public perception of the case. In a hallway outside the courtroom, he stood before a tangle of microphones and cameras and held an impromptu press conference in which he asserted that as a child, Caputo had been abandoned, raped, and beaten, that as a teenager he had been hospitalized in an Argentinian psychiatric institution and there declared schizophrenic, and that until recently he had been suffering as well from the newly popular psychiatric diagnosis, multiple-personality disorder. "He committed the murders while in the thrall of a psychotic personality," Kennedy declared, his deep voice filled with sympathy and awe, "and then managed to repress that personality."

"Why did Caputo choose this particular time to turn himself in?" one reporter asked.

"For a time he couldn't remember the killings," Kennedy replied. "But recently they came back to him. And they haunted him. He told me, 'I would rather have my body locked up and my mind free than go on living as I was, with my mind locked up and my body free.'"

"Are you going to argue that he's insane?" another reporter asked.

Kennedy's head bobbed toward him, but he answered the question only indirectly. "He belongs in a medical facility. A high-security medical facility."

In the next few days Caputo's image was everywhere, in newspapers, on TV news reports, and even, made up and carefully lighted, on the ABC newsmagazine show *PrimeTime Live*. The show was a dramatic scoop, a lengthy interview with the confessed killer, which, astonishingly, had been taped in Kennedy's office prior to the arraignment, prior even to the killer's surrender.

Like millions of Americans, I watched that show. I saw Caputo, neatly dressed in a blue-striped shirt, wrinkle his brow earnestly as the interviewer, Chris Wallace, plied him with prearranged questions, and heard him say, his words accented and his tone mournful, that he was sorry for what he'd done and had turned himself in because he recognized that he needed psychiatric help.

"Do you remember the day you killed Natalie?" Wallace asked. It was just after an unseen narrator had informed the audience that Caputo had alleged that Natalie had been becoming too possessive.

"I picked up a knife but I didn't know what I was going to do," Caputo replied. "I could hear the screams, and see her—partially. I was seeing stripes and lines, whites and reds and blues. And dots, a lot of dots."

"Were you aware that you were stabbing her?"

"No. I knew I was doing something bad, but I didn't know what I was doing."

Also on the show was a retired police detective, who explained that, in his view, "it was when Caputo was rejected that he killed these women." But most of the program was given over to Caputo's own explanations of why he had murdered and to an apologia offered by a woman to whom he was currently married and who had borne him four children. "During the ten years he lived with me, he was never aggressive," she said, as if to substantiate Kennedy's assertion that Caputo had several personalities. "The man who was married to me would never have harmed anyone."

The broadcast made television history. For one

thing, it offered an as yet unarrested killer the opportunity to explain himself before a national audience and thus gain the sympathy and even celebrity that could be useful to him once he went on trial. For another, at the end of the interview, a handful of New York State police who had been alerted by Kennedy that a long-hunted fugitive was ready to turn himself in (but not informed that if they took him into custody, their activities would be filmed) arrived in the lawyer's office and in a dazzle of lights "captured" Caputo. Such a moment had never before been televised.

The day after the *PrimeTime Live* show, and a week after I'd seen Caputo in the flesh for the first time, I saw him again at a second hearing in Mineola. Its purpose was the ordering of a psychiatric examination to determine whether he was competent to stand trial for the murder of Natalie Brown. He'd had such an examination back in 1971 and been judged incompetent.

Is the same thing going to happen this time? I wondered as I listened to the brief proceedings. It was that first ruling of incompetency, handed down twenty-three years ago, that had made it possible for Caputo to go on killing, for he hadn't been tried for Natalie's murder but instead been remanded to a psychiatric hospital. Psychiatric hospitals were, then and now, notoriously easy to elope from, and Caputo had escaped from his and gone on to murder the other three women whom he now admitted having killed. And maybe more, I thought. Maybe Jacqui.

I found Caputo even less appealing at this second hearing than I'd found him at the first. He was wearing a sharp leather jacket and the same not-unstylish blue-striped shirt he'd worn on television, but his clothes were rumpled and dirty as though he'd slept in them. His mouth was set into a hard, stony slash, the result, I assumed, of whatever medication he'd been placed on. And his onyx eyes, which had been glassy the first time I saw him, now looked altogether vacant.

I was making notes on his appearance when, to my surprise, he gave a nod to an attractive, even elegant, couple sitting in a front row. "It's the family," I overheard another reporter whisper to a colleague. "His brother. Alberto. And his sister-in-law. Kim. K-i-m." The handsome couple, who had come to court with Kennedy, were holding hands and looking nervous.

I knew a bit about Alberto and Kim Caputo by then, had found out that he owned a photography company in New York and that she was a writer and magazine editor who had previously been married to a psychoanalyst. But I'd made no effort to call them. I figured that if I phoned out of the blue and said, "Hello, I'm writing a book about Ricardo," I'd get nowhere. They'd refuse to say anything or, more likely, just hang up. But I could wait. Time was on my side. And maybe if I waited, I'd get someone, maybe Kennedy, to put in a good word for me with the Caputos, get them at least to take my call.

As I was musing, I saw that Ricardo was rising and being shackled by a pair of courtroom guards. The psychiatric examination had been ordered and the short hearing had ended. The guards led Ricardo out a back door and a moment later, Kennedy exited the well of the courtroom and began talking to Alberto and Kim. They huddled with him with their hands still entwined. And then Kennedy shepherded them out of the courtroom.

I tagged behind, saw the little group besieged by reporters and cameramen, and heard them beg the representatives of the media not to ask them ques-

tions but instead to read a statement that Kim
Caputo had composed. Then, as arms leaped
toward them like fish toward bread crumbs, they
handed out copies of a photocopied press release.

I reached for a copy, too. And found it unsettling,
for it seemed to blame society for neglecting
Ricardo, rather than Ricardo for transgressing society's rules. "Ricardo could have been helped long
ago and none of these deaths would have come to
pass," Kim Caputo, apparently convinced that psychiatry could heal all wounds, asserted. "He begged
for help many times and was left alone with his terrible illness and the devices that he created to deal
with the pain and abuse of his childhood. . . . He
turned himself in after committing his first murder
in Long Island and was treated so loosely that he
was on the street before two years were up. Not
once in twenty years did any authority question his
identity. He could walk on the streets of Hawaii like
a tourist. He was able to travel from one country to
another without being caught. The blood on his
hands, the screams in his head, the hallucinations
that blinded him from his deeds seemed to have
veiled him from the world. He not only was left
alone with his disease, he had become invisible."

The press release also attempted to answer the
question of why Ricardo had turned himself in at
this particular time. "We think it must be that the
love and support of his present wife has given him
the peace of mind," it speculated. "The comfort of
the relationship has made him visible again. His
conscience has returned."

He's visible all right, I said to myself, frowning as
I stood in the corridor and scanned the document.
But Natalie's invisible. Natalie and his other victims.

It wasn't just that they were dead. It was that they
were ciphers. Several newspapers had written about

them, but they'd been allotted just a short paragraph or two apiece.

Kennedy and the Caputos were leaving in a flurry of pursuing cameras. I went to the railroad, my mind bent on searching out people who might help me make Natalie Brown and Caputo's other victims visible.

3

By the time I began my research, Natalie's friends had scattered; her parents had died; so, too, had some of the law enforcement authorities who had worked on the case back in 1971. But eventually I found enough people who'd known Natalie to be able to get a sense of her. There was, for example, her brother Ed, the owner of a discount gift shop in North Carolina. "Nat—that was her nickname," he told me, "was really pretty. Looked just like Linda Blair in *The Exorcist*. And she was the apple of my parents' eyes. There were two boys, me and my brother, Bill, but Nat was the only girl."

Natalie had grown up in the suburban Long Island village of Flower Hill. She'd attended public schools there. And when she was a senior in high school, she decided that she wanted to go to college and afterward study nursing. "Our mother was a nurse," Ed explained, "and Natalie wanted to follow in her footsteps."

That year, 1969, she applied to and was accepted at Marymount College in Virginia, and after graduation, she did what so many graduating seniors do—spent a summer abroad. She toured through Italy, Germany, and Spain, writing ecstatic post-

cards to her friends back home in which she raved
about the amazing sites she was visiting. And about
the exciting young men she was meeting. "Dear
Chris," she wrote to one girlfriend in July 1969. "I'm
nervous, waiting for Stefano. My hands are shaking,
have not seen him." "Dear Chris," she wrote a few
days later. "Hi! Oh wow am I in love. Not Stefano. I
met the nicest guy—Czech." But despite her absorp-
tion in the adventure and romance of Europe, she
still intended to go to college and then study nursing, and when she returned home, she started at
Marymount.

She attended the school for nearly a year, but
Europe had given her a taste for freedom, and
toward the end of her second semester, she dropped
out. "She wanted to get a job and work for a while,"
Ed Brown said. "Not a whole long while. She would
have gone back to school, I'm sure of it. She just
wanted to save up some money and see what it was
like to be a working woman instead of a student."

What happened next, I learned from the police.
Natalie got her job, a position as a teller in a mid-
town-Manhattan branch of the Marine Midland
Bank. Caputo was working a few blocks away. The
son of an Argentinian woman and an Italian immigrant to Argentina, he'd emigrated to the United
States a year and a half earlier and was working in
New York as a hotel janitor, cleaning floors at the
Barbizon at night and washing walls at the Plaza in
the daytime. And one day in November 1970, he
went to Marine Midland to cash one of his Plaza
paychecks.

Natalie was standing behind her teller's window,
taking deposits, giving out cash. Ricardo, an inveter-
ate small-talker, struck up a conversation with her.

The following week Ricardo came to her window

again, and they chatted some more. Natalie found him appealing. But his English was not yet fluent and he didn't understand some of her words.

At that moment she made one of the most crucial decisions of her young life. She slipped Ricardo a note saying she'd like to get together with him sometime.

He was pleased and, wasting no time, invited her to go out with him that very night. Natalie accepted, and they ate dinner in a restaurant and saw a movie.

Several nights later Ricardo asked Natalie out on a second date and sometime that evening took her to see the small hotel room he was sharing with another Argentinian immigrant. His roommate was out and he and Natalie made love.

"That note," I said to a woman named Judy Epstein, who'd been one of Natalie's closest friends. "You know, when I first heard about it, I thought it was something Ricardo made up. That really it was he who made the first advance, who wrote Natalie a note. But the police say no."

"Oh, Natalie wrote the note all right," Judy said. The mother of two children, a twelve-year-old daughter and an eight-year-old son, she was thin and lithe, but her no longer perfect vision required glasses and her once-blond hair was iced with gray. "Natalie told me about the note, and I still remember that afterward, I said, 'Natalie! How could you! You don't even know him.' But Natalie just laughed at me and said, 'Well, he was cute.'"

Judy had grown up in New Jersey, but she lived now in a loft in bohemian lower Manhattan where, with her husband, she ran a musical-instrument repair shop. We were talking in that shop, an antiquated establishment that smelled of sawdust and varnish and whose rickety floors were weighted down by stacks of bass fiddles in various stages of decay or reconstruction.

"Natalie was bold," said Judy. "Once when she was in Europe, she met a guy she liked, and she went over to his house and left *him* a note. And she and some of her Flower Hill friends used to go down to the docks in Manhattan and pick up guys who were working on cruise ships. I loved her boldness. Because I was the cautious type, and not very happy about it. Whereas Natalie was one of these people who wanted to experience everything there was to experience in life. She wanted to eat up the world."

There was a big black backpack at Judy's feet and now she began rummaging in it. A moment later she extricated a photograph of Natalie, a black-and-white print set in an ornate inlaid frame. "Here, I brought you this. I keep it on my piano. Place of honor." She handed me the picture, and as she did so, her tone turned indignant. "Does this look like the sort of cloying woman who'd become so possessive you'd have to kill her to get rid of her? That's what they said on *PrimeTime Live* that Ricardo's been saying."

I could see why that allegation had angered her, for the picture showed a voluptuous teenager with a proud smile, long, flowing dark hair, and a majestic arms-akimbo, chest-forward stance. "That's Natalie?" I murmured. "I'd imagined her more delicate, more—overwhelmable."

"No. She was big. And strong. And one of the things I never understood was how Ricardo managed to overwhelm her. I guess it was because she was so innocent, so good-hearted, that violence was beyond her imagination. So her guard would have been completely down when Ricardo attacked her."

Judy was filled with memories of Natalie. How

they'd met at summer camp when they were little. Stayed friends throughout their teenage years. Curled up on one another's beds and talked late into the night about love and sex and life. Sprawled on the floor and listened to the Monkees—" 'I want to be free.' That was her favorite song," Judy said, " 'free like the warm September breeze.' "

"What about sex? Did she have much sexual experience before Ricardo?"

"Some. Guys liked her. She had these big breasts, and she was lighthearted, fun, the kind of girl who took all the dirt and guilt out of sex. But in a way, that's what made her vulnerable to Ricardo. There were always guys in her life, but all of them took her lightly. They didn't court her. Take her out. Want anything from her except fun."

"And Ricardo did?"

"He *told* her he did. And it made Natalie happy, at least at first. She'd always been looking for what she called 'real love.' And she'd always been complaining that no one took her seriously. Not her parents. Not boys. And now, suddenly she had this guy in her life who was saying not just 'I want you,' but 'I love you. I'm serious about you.' I think that was Ricardo's appeal. I think so because I could never see any other. And I thought about it a lot, even before he killed her."

Judy had thought about what Natalie found so appealing about Ricardo because she'd met him and been singularly unimpressed. "The three of us went walking around Greenwich Village one afternoon," she informed me. "And I remember not quite getting it—her and him. I mean, Natalie was bigger than life. And when she told me this guy was in love with her, I expected someone very special. Someone as imposing as she was. But Ricardo seemed sort of ordinary. I felt sad for her. I mean, not just me but all her friends were away at college that year. And she was working. In a boring bank job. And seeing this not very prepossessing guy. But he had told her he loved her, and that filled a void for her."

At this, Judy shook her head sadly. "It's so dangerous, this business of being a teenager. Sometimes I look at my daughter and I just wonder and wonder what's going on in her head now that her hormones are starting to kick in."

If Natalie had been eager to have a man claim to be serious about her, she had also been eager to convince her parents, her mother Julie, a nurse, and her father, Harold, an executive at a linen corporation, that she was capable of a serious relationship. And one day, not long after she'd started dating Ricardo, she took him home to meet her family.

Ed Brown remembered the occasion. "Ricardo was *nice*," he told me, emphasizing the word as if he was sure I would find it incomprehensible. "He was respectful, polite, even courtly. My mother and father liked him, and they told Natalie she could have him over anytime she liked."

That turned out to be frequently. "He came out most weekends," Ed said. "Natalie wasn't a hippie or a rebellious kid. I mean, she quit school, but she didn't go down and live in the East Village. She was a homebody. Liked to cook. Hang around the house. So she liked having Ricardo come out. And he liked it, too. He was living in a furnished room somewhere, and when you're living that way, it's nice being in a real home."

According to Ed, when Ricardo came to visit, he and Natalie were not overtly sexual. They slept in separate bedrooms and spent most of their time in childish pursuits, playing checkers and Monopoly, or watching TV.

But there was another side to their lives. Parties. Marijuana. An Argentinian man who once met Natalie and Ricardo at a party told me that he recalled that most of the guests that evening were turning on and growing ever more giddy and gigglish. But then something went wrong. "Ricardo got paranoid," he said. "He started yelling and screaming. Natalie was great. She kept trying to calm him and comfort him and talk him down. Sort of like a little mother."

"What about Ricardo?" I said. "What was he like when he wasn't high?"

"I don't know. I didn't know him well."

Few people did, according to a homicide detective I interviewed. "He didn't have friends. He had secrets," the detective, Ray Pierce, said to me.

"Secrets?"

"Yeah, after he killed Natalie, we spoke with a roommate of his, and we learned something very interesting." According to the roommate, when Ricardo first came to this country, he hung out in gay bars and gave sex for money and jewelry. And sometimes when he wasn't satisfied with what was offered, he'd rough up and rob his clientele.

Did Natalie know this? I doubt it, for in February 1971, when she had been dating Ricardo for three months, she went on a vacation with him, a vacation for which she paid both their expenses. They traveled first to Puerto Rico and the Virgin Islands, where they swam in the sapphire Caribbean and slept beneath palm trees in public campgrounds. Ricardo took pictures and Natalie wrote postcards, telling friends that she was being "eaten alive," presumably by the Caribbean beaches' notorious sand flies, and that she wasn't "as zonked as I used to be." When their Caribbean idyll was over, the pair impulsively decided not to return home. Ricardo wanted to see Florida and California, and Natalie agreed to accompany him. They visited Miami and Los Angeles, then made their way to San Francisco.

At the time it was a mecca for middle-class runaways, the legendary home of the hippies and flower children, and although the sixties were over, parts of the city were still filled with hucksters selling the accoutrements of the just vanished decade, its tie-dyed shirts and gauzy dresses, its beaded headbands, massage oil, peace symbols, and common and esoteric drugs.

Ricardo was intrigued by the scene, and so was Natalie, who agreed to take an apartment in San Francisco with him. No matter that she didn't have with her any apparel suitable for life in a nontropical climate. She called her parents and asked them to send her some of her clothes.

What did her parents think? They are dead and gone and there is no way to know for sure. But they were conventional people—"Depression babies for whom making a living was very important," Ed Brown had described them—and Natalie was their special joy. So I suspect that, like most parents whose children were lured to abandon their education or jobs by the siren songs of the time, they were exceedingly worried. And angry. They sent Natalie the clothing she requested. But they didn't send her any money—even though by then she was running out of it—and several weeks later, strapped for cash, Natalie decided to return to the East. Ricardo said he would, too, and they headed home, hitchhiking across the country.

On their return, Ricardo began insisting to Natalie that they get married. His visa had expired,

but if she married him, he explained, he could
remain in the United States. Natalie, who was living at home once again, went down to an office of
the Immigration and Naturalization Service and
filled out papers saying Ricardo, too, was living at
her Flower Hill address, and that they were
engaged.

But something had changed. Natalie, who may
have seen during their travels too much of the
angry, touchy side of her lover, began to sour on
Ricardo. One day, she told him she was pregnant,
but not long afterward she visited a doctor and
returned with the news that she wasn't pregnant
after all. Or anymore. Another day, she wrote to a
friend that she was considering going back to a previous boyfriend. And throughout the spring, despite
what she had told immigration officials, she said
nothing to her family about being engaged to
Ricardo or even about wanting to marry him.

"I doubt she ever had any real intention of doing
so," Ed Brown told me. "My parents wouldn't have
objected. They liked Ricardo a lot. But my father
was a self-made man, an executive who'd started
out in his company as a traveling salesman. He
would have wanted Ricardo to have a good job
before he married Natalie, would have offered him
one in his firm, and that simply never came up."

Nor did Natalie tell her friends that she was
engaged to or going to marry Ricardo. Indeed, as
spring turned to summer, she began complaining
about him. Early in June she went swimming at
Taconic State Park with Judy Epstein and two male
friends, buddies from their old summer camp, and
when one of the men told her she looked sensation-
al in her little black bikini, she said, "Don't ever let
Ricardo hear you say that! He's terrifically jealous."
Later that month, she told a neighbor who often

dropped by to visit her that he'd better stop doing so because his presence made Ricardo angry. And in July she repeatedly told one of her old boyfriends, a fellow named Jim Gay, that Ricardo was getting on her nerves because he was always making demands on her.

I was curious about those demands, and one day I managed to locate Jim Gay. Nowadays, he makes his home in a spacious, neat-as-a-pin house on Long Island's opulent "Gold Coast," and he's a banker and the father of two adolescents. But in the days he knew Natalie, he lived near her in Flower Hill and, an adolescent himself, played the electronic organ in a rock band.

Jim and Natalie had dated during their junior and senior years of high school, and Natalie had often gone to hear Jim and his band play. Then they'd broken up, gone off to college, and stopped seeing each other. But in the summer of 1971, Jim was home from school and, like Natalie, working in Manhattan. "That summer, she and I used to commute home together from our jobs," he explained. "Not every day. But whenever we could. We'd meet in Penn Station and ride back out to the Island together. And sometimes when we did, she'd talk to me about Ricardo."

"What did she say about him?" I asked.

"That he was asking her for things all the time."

"What kinds of things?"

"Money. I guess he thought she was a rich American, that all Americans were rich. Anyway, Natalie didn't like it. And she complained about it to me several times. Even mentioned it the last time I saw her, which was a day or two before she was killed. We'd met at Penn Station, and on the way home, she talked about how he was still asking her

for money. And then, she said something new.
Something she hadn't said before."

"What was it?" I was impatient to know.

"That she didn't have the time or patience for
Ricardo anymore and was going to end the relationship. I still remember her words. She said, 'I've
already told him I want to break up with him. But it
didn't seem to register. So next time I see him, I'm
going to lay down the law.' "

At this, Jim sighed, a long, loud sigh. "You know,
it's funny, after all these years, but I remember being
so pleased when she said that. I still liked her, and I
guess I figured that if she broke up with Ricardo,
maybe she and I might get together again. So I invited her to come hear the band on the weekend. We
had a gig at a neighborhood bar, both Friday and
Saturday nights. 'For old times' sake,' I said. And
Natalie said, 'Great. Maybe Saturday. I don't think
Ricardo will still be around by Saturday.' And I
felt"—Jim paused, the sound of his breath once
again heavy—"terrific. That's what I felt. She was
the kind of girl who could make you feel terrific just
thinking you were going to see her."

Shortly after Natalie told Jim Gay she was going
to break up with her Argentinian suitor, Ricardo
came out to Flower Hill for another weekend, arriving on Friday evening, July 30, 1971. Natalie may
have meant to do what she'd told Jim she was going
to do, may have intended to lay down the law and
get Ricardo to leave. But her parents and brothers
were home when he arrived; she and Ricardo slept
in their separate rooms, and on Saturday, when she
might have hoped to grab a few minutes of private
conversation with him, her mother asked for her
help in preparing the family's meals. Natalie bided
her time. Her parents and brothers would be going

out in the evening, she knew, and she could talk to
Ricardo then. So she assisted Julie in the kitchen,
then played a long game of Monopoly with Ricardo.
And when he tired of playing, she turned on the TV
and watched a Marx Brothers movie with him.

Ed Brown joined them in front of the set. He
noticed that Ricardo seemed to be having a fine
time, laughing spiritedly at the jokes he got and asking eagerly for explanations of the ones he couldn't
fathom. Then Ed took off for his job as a nighttime
cab dispatcher. And everyone else, except for
Natalie and Ricardo, took off, too, Bill for a date
with a girlfriend, Harold and Julie for a friend's
anniversary celebration.

As soon as Natalie and Ricardo were finally
alone, according to a confession Ricardo later dic-
tated to the police, they went upstairs to Natalie's
bedroom, a room still furnished with stuffed bears,
plush monkeys, and other childhood treasures but
adorned with more womanly trophies, too, with
posters from Natalie's trip to Italy and a portrait of
her that Ricardo, who fancied himself an artist, had
drawn and presented to her. When they entered the
room, Ricardo wanted to make love. But Natalie, he
confessed, rejected his advances. Perhaps she said
merely that it was because she wanted to break up
with him. Or perhaps she said what he claimed she
did, which was that she had been making love with
someone else. In any event, she turned aside his
embraces and, leaving the bedroom, went down-
stairs and outside onto a porch.

He followed her there, he explained to the police,
and said calmly, "I thought you wanted to marry
me." And he only got mad, he further explained,
when she left the porch, went into the kitchen, and,
seeing him behind her, pushed him away and called
him a "fucking spic."

Maybe. But some of the detectives who heard his confession thought, based on their years of experience with similar cases, that most likely he had become enraged as soon as she turned down his sexual offer, and that when she traveled from bedroom to porch to kitchen, she was already trying to fend him off.

Certainly, in the kitchen she was like a cornered animal. Ricardo chased her and caught up with her in front of the stove, grabbed a long, thin kitchen knife her mother used for boning fish, and began stabbing her. She got away for a second and scurried toward the sink. But he caught up with her and stabbed her some more. And some more. And when she fell down, her legs sprawled beneath her and her eyes staring up at him, he got down, too, and, dropping the knife, put his hands around her throat and held them there, tightened them there, until her jerking body went still. Then he got up, saw that his shirt was drenched with blood, took it off, put on a sweater, and, carrying the shirt, fled from the house.

It was dark and silent on the suburban streets. Ricardo raced down them and, passing a gas station, tossed the bloody shirt into one of the station's trash cans. But after that, that first time, he didn't know what else to do, where he might go. He stood in the shadows for a while and then, not yet the escape artist he would one day become, went to the gas station's phone booth, dialed 911, and said, "I've just killed my girlfriend."

Minutes later, the police arrested him.

"What else did Caputo say that night?" I asked Detective William Coningsby, who had been one of the first police officers on the crime scene and who had later taken down Caputo's confession. Coningsby had retired and was living in Myrtle

Beach, South Carolina, and I'd flown down there to
interview him. A suntanned golfer, he'd met me at
the airport, showed me around the town, and
regaled me with Myrtle Beach arcana such as the
story of the ghostly Gray Man who is said to haunt
the powdery strands at dusk. Then he'd driven me to
his home, a peaceful haven on the edge of a golf
course.

"Well, Caputo certainly didn't say anything like
what he said on that *PrimeTime Live* show,"
Coningsby began, offering me a seat on a screened
porch. "He *knew* why he'd killed Natalie Brown.
One of our guys, an officer named Lawrence Miron,
was one of the people who arrested him. He was
sent to pick Ricardo up at the gas station, and he
and his partner put him in their car and drove with
him to Natalie's house. Then, Miron went into the
house. He saw what was in there, and he came back
out and asked Caputo why he'd killed the girl who
was lying in the kitchen. And Ricardo said it was
because she was in love with someone else."

Coningsby had a file on his lap, and he opened it
and began leafing through it. "Here. Miron went
into the Browns' house, leaving Ricardo out in the
car with his partner. He saw Natalie's body, came
out, and told his partner that it was true, someone
had indeed been murdered. And Ricardo said, 'Kill
me.' So Miron said, 'Why?' And Ricardo said,
'Because I think I killed her.' And then Miron asked
him why he'd killed her. And he said what I told you.
He said, 'Because she loves another.' "

"And now he's saying she didn't?"

"Well, you heard him. He's saying she was possessive, wanted him to marry her. I guess he forgot
what he said the first time around. But he didn't say
it just to Miron. He said it to me, too."

Turning pages in his file, Coningsby pulled out a

copy of the written confession he had elicited from
Ricardo. " 'My name is Ricardo Silvio Caputo,' " he
read. " 'I slept over on Friday in the TV room. . . .
Bill and Edward went out. . . . Natalie's mother and
father also went out. Natalie took me by the hand
and we went upstairs to her room. . . . I tried to
make love to her, she pushed me away, and said, "I
do not want to make love to you because I've been
making love with someone else." ' "

The discrepancy between what Ricardo had said
right after he killed Natalie and what he had been
saying since he had turned himself in was dramatic. But I was even more fascinated by something
else Coningsby read to me later from Ricardo's confession. It was a section in which Ricardo had
talked about the early days of his relationship with
Natalie. "She always wanted to make love," he'd
said. "I had to quit my night job because she was
always in my room after four P.M."

Those sentences struck me as bizarre. He's blaming *his* quitting work on *her* sexual appetites, I
thought when I heard them. He sees female sexuality as voracious. And failure-inducing. It was my
first clue to his psyche, my first insight into the
exact nature of his hatred toward women.

4

While I was researching Natalie's story, Caputo was examined by a court-appointed psychiatrist. He concluded that Ricardo was not psychiatrically ill but merely feigning illness and ruled him mentally competent to stand trial for Natalie's murder. Additionally, a Nassau County assistant district attorney named Elise McCarthy was assigned to prosecute the case.

"Do you have any contacts in Argentina?" she said to me one afternoon in September. I'd spoken to her on the phone several times, but this was our first face-to-face meeting, an interview in a dimly lit conference room where the table was pitted with scratches and the ripped upholstered chairs displayed not just their stuffing but their springs.

"Maybe," I answered, though what I was thinking of was a long shot. "I have a friend whose husband does business in Argentina. Maybe he knows someone—though I'm sure you have better contacts than him."

"Not necessarily. At least, my contacts haven't been able to get me what I want." I was pleased that she was asking for my help. Getting information is always easier if you can provide information. "What is it you want?" I asked.

"The source of a newspaper story," McCarthy said, and launched into a curious tale. "*Clarín*, the leading Buenos Aires newspaper, printed a story about Ricardo right after he turned himself in which asserted that, contrary to what he's been saying about his surrender—which by the way has always seemed like pure crap to me—he didn't come in out of the cold because he felt remorse but because he *had* to give himself up. Someone was on to him for something."

"That sure puts things in a different light," I said.

"You bet." McCarthy pulled a photocopy out of a manila folder she'd been balancing on her lap and looked down at it. "How's your Spanish?"

"So-so."

"That's better than mine." Reaching across the sorry table, she handed me the document, a newspaper clipping from *Clarín*. "*Ricardo Caputo confesó,*" I read, "*que el 18 de enero en el aeropuerto de la Ciudad de México, fue detenido por cuatro policías que lo buscaban por un quinto homicidio.*" Ricardo Caputo confessed that on January 18 at the Mexico City airport he was stopped by four police officers who were looking for him regarding a fifth homicide.

The photocopy was muddy and blurred and I struggled over the words, but in the end I made out most of the article. Its gist was that according to Ricardo, after the police stopped him, they took him to a room in the airport and interrogated him, upon which he volunteered the information that he had a substantial sum of money in a local bank. This suggestion of a bribe, again according to Ricardo, prompted the officers to escort him to his bank, where he withdrew and gave them money, after which he returned to the airport and boarded a plane bound for Argentina.

"Where'd *Clarín* get this information?" I asked, stunned at the difference between this account of why Ricardo had fled Mexico for Argentina and the one he'd given on television, which was that his flight had been sparked not by pursuit but remorse.

"That's what I want to know." McCarthy pointed a scarlet fingertip at the top of the article. "They attribute the story to Ricardo. But who did he tell it to?" Her voice rose with annoyance. "As you can see, there's no byline. And when I had one of our people call down there, no one would say who their source was, or even who wrote the story."

"What makes you think I'll fare better?"

"Maybe you won't. But it's worth some more digging, and I don't have the money, the resources."

Money and resources were very much on McCarthy's mind that day. "Kennedy is probably going to plead Caputo not guilty by reason of insanity," she said, "and in an insanity case, everything matters. Not just what Caputo did here in Nassau County, but what he did everywhere else he lived over the past twenty-three years. And I don't have the help. I've had to make the most basic phone calls on my own."

McCarthy, who appeared to be in her late thirties, was a handsome woman with a statuesque figure, deep blue eyes, and long, glossy black hair. A graduate of St. John's Law School in Queens, New York, she'd been working in the Nassau County DA's office for eleven years, the last six in the Major Offense Bureau, where she'd handled a number of high-profile cases. But never one as complex as this, she told me, explaining, "Part of the problem is that it's so old. Some of our witnesses have died. And some of the 1971 records have disappeared. We don't even have a transcript of the hearing that found Caputo not competent. We think it burned up in a warehouse fire."

I nodded. I'd been having difficulties, too.

"But there's one thing that pleases me," McCarthy went on. "Caputo's been given another psychiatric examination, this time by the defense. It's all on videotape—and guess who conducted the examination."

"Beats me." I shrugged.

"Dr. Park Elliott Dietz! You know, the guy they call Witness for the *Prosecution,* because that's which side he generally works for. I can't imagine why Kennedy chose him, except that Kennedy must like celebrities. Because Dietz isn't like some of these doctors who'll say anything to satisfy whoever's paying their bills. He has a stipulation in his contracts that says he's there to find the truth, and not necessarily to find for the party who's hired him. So maybe we'll get lucky. Maybe he won't find Caputo insane."

We talked a bit about Dietz, about how he'd examined John Hinckley and helped put away Jeffrey Dahmer, and then I switched the subject to Jacqui Bernard. "Do you think Caputo killed her, too?"

"Not just her," McCarthy said, "but maybe even another woman as well. A woman in Los Angeles. She worked with Caputo in the early 1980s, and during the time they worked together, she was found murdered."

"The early 1980s! Caputo's been saying he stopped killing back in 1977."

McCarthy opened the folder on her lap and looked down at a piece of paper. "Well, this woman was killed in 1981. Two years before Jacqui Bernard. She was a waitress or a cook at the Scandia restaurant. And he was a waiter there."

I was fascinated by the coincidence. But confused. "If Caputo killed her, why wouldn't he say so? I mean, here he's turning himself in and admitting he's killed four people. What's another two to him?"

McCarthy shrugged. "I don't know. But I don't have to know."

I couldn't let it go. "Could it be that he's saying he had nothing to do with that killing because it happened after California reinstated the death penalty? Could that be a factor?"

"Anything's possible," McCarthy said. "But the most likely explanation is that the murders which Caputo has admitted are all murders where there's absolutely no doubt that he did the killing. Murders where he was known to have been involved with the victims, had been seen with them by their friends and families. Jacqui Bernard's case was different. She didn't introduce her friends and family to Caputo—but maybe she liked to keep her love life to herself. And this L.A. woman, she wasn't known to have any relationship with him except for working in the same place he did. But maybe she was a private person, too. Or maybe she went out with him just once—*that* once."

I was puzzled. "Are you saying Caputo may be a true serial killer? That he didn't kill only women with whom he'd had long-standing relationships?"

"It's one of the theories we have," McCarthy nodded. "But it's going to be hard to tie him to any killings to which he hasn't confessed. Because it's all so long ago. And there wasn't much evidence to go on in the first place. Not with Jacqui, and not with this L.A. woman, either. He wasn't even questioned in her death."

McCarthy, who had earlier mentioned that she was a keen victim's advocate, sounded discouraged. I got the feeling she wanted passionately to see

Caputo put into prison for the rest of his life and
was worried that it might not happen, worried that
for all her hopes about Dietz, a jury might find
Caputo not guilty by reason of insanity. Or guilty of
manslaughter, rather than murder. And indeed, a
few minutes later, she said as much to me. "I envy
the folks up in Westchester," she sighed. "Because
their case, the Judith Becker case, is clearly murder.
This one is trickier. It's got elements of extreme
emotional distress. I mean, Caputo *did* call the
police right after he killed Natalie."

As soon as I was home, I phoned my friend
whose husband did business in Argentina. "Does
your husband know anyone connected with the
press in Buenos Aires?" I asked.

"I guess so," Naomi replied. "He knows this
lawyer who knows *everyone*."

"Great," I said, and asked her to ask her husband
to ask his contact to try to get the information from
Clarín that McCarthy had wanted.

What happened afterward was odd. Naomi called
back a few days later and said that the lawyer with
whom her husband did business in Argentina had
telephoned one of the top editors at the paper, a
person he knew well. He'd asked about the source of
the puzzling story and the editor had said, "Funny,
someone else wanted to know that, too. But we
couldn't help. We don't know."

"Well, could I talk to whoever wrote the story?"
the lawyer had asked. And the editor had said, "It
wasn't written here. We got it from the AP."

I called the Associated Press after that and tried to
find out who at the wire service had filed the story.
But after numerous phone calls and the filling out of
forms, I was informed that the story had not
emanated from AP. "It must have been *Clarín*'s own

stuff," a perplexed but patient AP employee declared.

It was back to square one—except that now I suspected that *Clarín* was protecting its source. I told this to McCarthy, who said, "Damn. I *know* he didn't turn himself in because all of a sudden what he did to those poor dead women started preying on his mind. But I sure wish we could prove it."

Besides looking for elusive Argentinian sources, I was also trying at that time to find out whether the New York police were going to question Ricardo about the death of Jacqui Bernard. To that end I spoke with the detective who'd been put in charge of the case. He was Jerry Giorgio, a famous Manhattan detective who had unraveled a great many of the city's more puzzling murders and was said to have an extraordinary ration of perseverance.

When I called Giorgio, he told me that Michael Kennedy had informed him that Caputo categorically denied any involvement in Jacqui's murder. "He says he stopped killing back in the seventies," Giorgio said, "and that besides, he was working in L.A. at the time she was killed."

But had the police themselves talked with Caputo, I wanted to know. Not yet, Giorgio informed me. "We asked Kennedy to let us speak to him, and first he was going to, and then he said no, not unless you provide us with a list of questions. We didn't want to do that, because it's no good. They have your questions, they can shape the answers."

"So what happens next?"

"Well, we've given Kennedy a list of dates and he's supposed to give us a list of where Caputo was on those dates. But it hasn't been forthcoming. So at the moment, you'd have to say things are up in the air."

I said I'd stay in touch and shifted my focus to

Westchester County, where Caputo's second admitted victim, Judith Becker, had been killed. I interviewed the county's charismatic district attorney, Jeanine Pirro, who told me, "We're going to try Caputo for murder. We're actively putting together our case."

She was a small woman, or at least she seemed small, sitting in an extravagantly high-backed, maroon leather chair in front of an enormous desk. But her eyes were huge, ashy brown and long-lashed, and when she spoke, they seemed to light up with an inner fire. "Caputo's not dissimilar to Scott Douglas," she said, referring to a major case she'd recently had, Douglas's murder of his wife, newspaper heiress Anne Scripps. "He, too, would cajole women and persuade them that he was a man of sensitivity. And then he would become insecure and worried about his position, and he'd take out his insecurities on whoever was the current woman in his life. There are a lot of men like that out there."

The Simpson trial had not yet started, but it was very much on Pirro's mind. "There are more men like Douglas and O.J. and Caputo out there than people realize," she went on, eyes blazing. And she went even further. "If you look at homicide statistics, you see that women who are murdered are overwhelmingly murdered by men they know well. Caputo's fascinating because he killed not just one but at least four women who knew him well. But he's just an extreme example of the kind of man who imagines that once a woman gets involved with him, he owns her and consequently is entitled to do whatever he wants with her—even take her life."

"Do you have a good case against Caputo?" I asked, thinking of McCarthy.

"I believe so," Pirro said, "though the fact that it happened twenty years ago creates problems." The light in her eyes went off as she spun out a depressing scenario. "We'll have trouble putting it together. Witnesses have moved or died. Police officers have retired. Memories have faded. The case'll have all those nightmares prosecutors hate."

But a moment later the light was back. "Twenty years ago. Thirty years ago. It doesn't matter how long ago a murder happened. A victim must never be forgotten." She had recharged herself right there in front of my eyes and was letting me know that whatever the difficulties, the Becker case was going to be pursued vigorously.

5

Becker. Her story was altogether different from Natalie's. She was no rebel, no adventure-seeking teenager. Twenty-six years old when Caputo killed her, she'd been a psychologist, a respected staff member at New York's Matteawan State Hospital for the Criminally Insane. "Tell me about her," I said to her sister, Janie Becker, one day.

"Judith was intelligent, hardworking, and idealistic," Janie, her elder by two years, said. At the time, we were standing in a corridor of the Westchester County courthouse, and as I looked at Janie, who was dressed in pearls, a flowered print dress, and spotless white sandals, I felt certain I knew what Judith would have looked like if she, too, had reached her forties. Like a suburban matron. Like a woman you see lunching at a tea shop where the window curtains are tied back with sashes and the tables are adorned with tiny vases of flowers.

The pair of them, Judith and Janie, had grown up in Bridgewater, Connecticut, a quiet, pristine town that seems almost the quintessential example of the America city dwellers like me dream of when we imagine life must somewhere be better than it is where we live, a town with a village green, colonial houses, gleaming white churches, huge shade trees, and neighbors who not only know each other's names but family histories as well. Their parents were Catholic and community-minded. When they were youngsters, their mother, Jane, worked as a secretary at the parochial school to which they were sent, and their father, Henry, was elected first selectman of Bridgewater, the equivalent of mayor. The girls grew up loving music, and especially the musicales their parents were fond of giving, lively neighborly evenings at which Jane served home-baked cakes and Henry entertained by caroling old-fashioned songs such as "In the Gloaming" and "Beautiful Dreamer."

Janie had been the more sparkling sister, I learned from friends of Judith's. At the high school both girls attended, New Milford High, Janie had been a star, a cheerleader, whereas Judith had been shy. "Almost painfully shy," a woman named Alanna Keating, who had gone to high school with the two of them, remembered. "New Milford High had a dress code, buttoned-up shirts and short hair for the boys, skirts that came down below the knees for the girls. But Judith's skirts were the longest. Her blouses were really demure. And she almost never went out on dates." But she was good-natured, well liked by both boys and girls. And she was smart. "Her best friend was the class genius," Alanna commented.

Judith's shyness abated somewhat during her college years, which she spent at Central Connecticut State. There, her intellect impressed several professors, one of whom, noting that she was altruistic and longed to better the lives of people less fortunate than herself, suggested she pursue a career in psychology.

Judith took his advice and, intending one day to

work with disadvantaged children, enrolled in a master's degree program in clinical psychology at St. John's University in Queens, New York. While studying, she lived on her own in an apartment near the school, had a few boyfriends, and became a little more sophisticated. But she remained, essentially, a reserved and unworldly young woman with a generous but somewhat unrealistic view of both life and the reaches of her profession. When she completed her degree and, instead of holding out for a job that would allow her to work with children, took the position at Matteawan, she told a friend that she was convinced that with her newly won arts and skills, she could save *anyone*.

Ricardo was at Matteawan. Detective Coningsby, when I'd visited him at Myrtle Beach, had told me how he'd come to be there. "You know, Ricardo had seemed perfectly normal to me the night I took his confession about Natalie," Coningsby had said. "I mean, as normal as a person can be after killing someone. He knew just what he'd done and why he'd done it. It was only later that anyone thought he might be nuts."

"And why was that?" I'd asked, making my notes with difficulty, for at that point we'd been talking so long on Coningsby's screened porch that it was nearly evening.

"Because he began talking to Natalie," Coningsby had replied. "Because he began saying things like 'Natalie, I love you so much' and 'Natalie, when are we going to get together?' sounding like he didn't realize she was dead."

I'd shivered when Coningsby said this, and I'm not sure whether it was because the shadowy gray air had turned the porch cold or because, in the approaching dusk of this region of specters and

ghost stories, I was finding it eerie to think of
Ricardo talking to his dead girlfriend. But whatever
it was, Coningsby had taken it for the latter and he'd
laughed at me, a booming, cheerful laugh. "It was a
ploy," he'd said. "Caputo had gotten some jailhouse
education, had heard he might be better off if he
pretended to be insane. So he started acting crazy—
acting, mind you."

That was the police theory back in 1971. But
when Ricardo's conversations with the dead Natalie
hadn't abated, the Nassau County district attorney's
office had had him examined and tested by a team
of court-appointed psychiatrists. They'd found him
pleasant and cooperative but disoriented—he'd stated among other things that the month was
February, when in fact it was August. They'd also
found his emotional reactions inappropriate and
his grasp of reality shaky. He'd smiled and seemed
quite happy, and he'd spoken as if not just Natalie
was still alive, but even his father, who had been
dead for more than a dozen years. "My father isn't
good to me," he'd said. "But Natalie is going to help
me with that. She's very nice. She comes to see me
in jail." And when his interviewers had informed
him firmly that Natalie and his father were dead,
he'd allowed that it was possible that he was hearing voices and confessed that he'd heard voices
before, had been so plagued by them when he was a
teenager that he'd voluntarily committed himself to
an Argentinian mental hospital. The psychiatrists
charged with examining him concluded he was
"suffering from a severe mental illness" that was
most likely schizophrenia, and shortly thereafter, a
judge remanded him not for trial but to Matteawan.
    There, at the dreary, antiquated hospital for the
criminally insane, he continued at first to act dis-

oriented and to hallucinate about Natalie's coming
to see him. He also expressed paranoid ideas,
blamed his father for all that had happened to him.
And he spoke about being depressed and wanting to
commit suicide. But within weeks of his arrival, he
showed signs of improvement, mingling with other
patients, boasting about his artistic talents, and asking repeatedly for special treatment. "Patient is very
demanding," observed one Matteawan staff member. "Patient shows manipulative tendencies in his
manner of responding to questions and answers,"
observed another.

In the light of these characteristics, several
Matteawan psychiatrists began to suspect that
Ricardo was a dissembler, a con artist, a shrewd
man pretending to a sickness he didn't have. And
they began to theorize that rather than being schizophrenic, as the court-appointed psychiatrists
who'd examined him previously had concluded,
Ricardo was suffering from an antisocial personality disorder—that he was what used to be called a
psychopath but is today more commonly known as
a sociopath.

Sociopathy is not a condition that can be used to
argue insanity in a criminal case. Nor is it a treat-
able condition. No psychotherapies or psychophar-
macological drugs can eradicate it. Still, his case
periodically reviewed by judges who periodically
ruled that he should be kept at Matteawan, Ricardo
remained at the hospital, where he was given occasional counseling and psychological testing. And
thus it was that in the fall of 1973, when he had
been at Matteawan close to two years, he met Judith
Becker, who had just joined the staff.

A fellow worker remembered what she was like
at the time. "She was sweet," he told me. "And very

natural in her dress and demeanor. She wore clothes that weren't flashy, shoes that were sensible. In fact, sensible was the chief impression she conveyed."

She appeared so sensible, and her training was so impeccable, that she was assigned to the hospital's most dangerous ward, the one that housed violent patients. But Judith wasn't fazed. She went about her tasks, chiefly the administering of psychological tests to the inmates, with seriousness and dedication, and in September 1973, she was assigned to test Ricardo.

She had read his case history by that time, had learned that he had once killed a girlfriend. But she liked him, viewed him as more intelligent, more courteous, more rehabilitable than other patients. Soon after she tested him, she visited his ward with some other female staff members and, music lover that she was, brought him a record player. But she didn't have much of a chance to get to know Ricardo. In a few weeks, he was transferred to a different, less guarded facility, Manhattan State Hospital on Wards Island.

The decision to transfer Ricardo was not Judith's. He was one of some five hundred mentally disturbed New York prisoners who were ordered into more loosely supervised hospitals because of two judicial decisions. The first was a U.S. Supreme Court decision. The high court had ruled that defendants considered insane could be kept in close confinement only if found dangerous by a jury. The second, a New York State decision, had ruled that defendants who were incompetent to stand trial could not be held at Matteawan until their cases had been adjudicated.

This loosening of the rules regarding mentally disturbed defendants was part and parcel of other, vast changes regarding mental illness that were sweeping through American society in the early 1970s. Everywhere, largely as a result of powerful and efficient new drug therapies, psychiatric hospitals were being shut down, patients were being released into their communities, and the very notion of insanity as a stigma and an incurable condition was being overhauled.

Ricardo was simply a beneficiary of this optimistic climate of opinion. But he said a happy farewell to Matteawan and to Judith, who promised to come see him at his new institution.

Judith was true to her word. Sometime in the midautumn of 1973 she visited Ricardo at Wards Island, where she learned he was behaving like a model patient, working in the hospital cafeteria and in his spare time drawing portraits of his fellow inmates. Her optimistic view of him confirmed, she asked the hospital administrators if she could take him on an outing—Wards Island inmates were not only permitted to roam the hospital grounds freely but were frequently given passes to leave the facility altogether—and her request was granted.

On that first outing she took Ricardo to dinner and to see a cowboy movie. And on another day she took him to see the new apartment in which she was living. It was in Yonkers, about a forty-five-minute drive from Wards Island, a small apartment, but one she had furnished tastefully. In the living room there was a flowered rug, a few rattan chairs, a spacious glass cocktail table, and a soft upholstered couch. In the bedroom there was a bed covered with a cozy quilt of crocheted squares.

Judith and Ricardo lay down on that bed one night, and Judith, the sexual side of herself long contained and given little expression, was enthralled by Ricardo's lovemaking.

At Christmas she sent him an appreciative greeting card, a card that was at once childish and suggestive. On the outside, there was Santa, listening to the whisperings of a cartoon figure, and the message:

YOU SHOULD GET A LOT OF PRESENTS THIS CHRISTMAS. I TOLD SANTA THAT YOU HAVE BEEN GOOD **ALL YEAR!**

On the inside, the message read:

FORTUNATELY
I DIDN'T TELL HIM AT **WHAT**

She signed it "Judy."

Their relationship intensified in the next two months. Judith frequently drove down from Yonkers to Wards Island, picked Ricardo up at the mental hospital, and took him home to her apartment, where they made love. But their lovemaking was not always a happy experience for her. Ricardo, even when he was at his most seductive, did something in bed that unnerved her. He liked to tickle her, no doubt making her squirm and wriggle. But she tried to grow used to it. She had come to believe she was in love with him.

In February, just before she left town on a brief vacation to Puerto Rico, she mailed him a love letter, one of several she was eventually to send him. In a neat hand, using her prim, personalized, blue-edged stationery and addressing him as "Ritchie," she wrote, "I'll miss talking with you, looking at you, making love with you. But I won't miss the tickling!

Yeah, I guess in a way I'll miss even that. Every time I see you . . . I feel closer to you." She signed it "Love, Judy." And soon, she began not just sleeping with Ricardo, but introducing him to her friends. She never told them exactly who he was. She said he was a coworker of hers, a colleague who worked at the psychiatric hospital on Wards Island.

She also encouraged him to write poetry. And he did. Love poems. In one, he alluded to having a secret self, but implied that Judith's love for him was making it fade away:

> "Love" that pulls at me . . .
> peeks
> At that inner me
> That's hiding . . .
> hesitating, I slowly
> Reach out.

In another poem, he warned her that she'd best not expect too much from him and revealed a certain touchiness about being argued with or slighted:

> Please don't expect me
> To always be good and kind and loving
> There are times when I will be cold and
> Thoughtless and hard to understand
>
> But it will only be because of the weather
> Or the flu
> Or one of my moods . . .
>
> Please listen to me when I'm talking to you
> and please
> Don't ever think about someone else
> When I kiss you.
> Please don't start an argument

Or make me look foolish
In front of other people . . .

Judith treasured the poetry and saved it all, no doubt believing that through her love and good offices, she might tame and even ennoble him. Psychoanalysts call such notions rescue fantasies, and they are particularly common among the kind-hearted.

Judith may also have been having different sorts of fantasies, masochistic sexual fantasies. Certainly Ricardo would claim when he turned himself in years after his romance with Judith that not only had she had such fantasies but that she had demanded that he act them out with her. Indeed, he would report that he had been so concerned about Judith's favorite sexual activities that he had discussed them with a Manhattan State Hospital psychologist, informing him that what Judith asked for in bed was for him to slap her around, plunge his penis roughly into her delicate anus, even put a knife to her writhing body while she masturbated. "You ought to stop seeing her," he would recall the psychologist's having said. "Maybe she's suicidal. But whatever she is, she's playing with a loaded .45."

But did Ricardo have such a conversation with a psychologist? No record of it was ever found in the notes of any psychologist who saw him at Manhattan State. And whether or not he had such a conversation, at whose urging might the dangerous sexual games he described have taken place—if they did take place? In the early 1970s a proliferation of sexual advice books had promulgated the sharing and acting out of fantasies as a means of establishing sexual bliss and emotional good health. I suppose it's possible that Judith could have been gullible enough to pursue this dubious fleshly Holy Grail with a man she knew to have been a murderer. But it seems to me far more likely that it was Ricardo who yearned for and practiced sadistic sex. Maybe he's the one who longs for cruelty in bed, I thought when I first heard his account of Judith's sexual tastes. Maybe he's projecting, and revealing the perverse dramas that were swirling around in *his* head at the time. Because women may have fantasies about cruel sex, but it's the rare woman indeed who desires to have those fantasies made real.

Judith and Ricardo saw each other regularly well into the spring of 1974. But in the summer Judith, just like Natalie three years earlier, decided she wanted to end the relationship. She had ample reasons. For one thing, Ricardo had turned more unpredictable than he'd been in the beginning of their relationship. He had taken to walking off the grounds of his casually guarded hospital whenever he chose and showing up at her apartment without letting her know he was coming. For another, he had turned moodier. When he arrived unexpectedly, if he discovered she was not free to spend time with him because she had made plans with other people, he would fly into a tantrum. He'd even get angry when the plans she'd made were to see her family.

But the most compelling reason may have been that Judith had become pregnant. She told a friend that Ricardo was the father of the child growing within her, but she didn't say anything to Ricardo about it. And despite her religious upbringing, she began to consider having an abortion, no doubt fearing that if she didn't, she might be saddled to her child's father forever.

Not long afterward, on a sunny July Saturday, Ricardo turned up without prior notice at her apartment. Judith told him she was on her way to her parents' house in Connecticut. But he demanded that she take him along, and Judith, perhaps afraid of his temper, acquiesced. With him at her elbow, she telephoned her mother and said, "Hi, Mom, my friend Ritchie is here and I was wondering if I could bring him up with me." Jane Becker, not knowing who Ritchie was or what her daughter's feelings about him were, said yes.

Later that morning the two arrived in Bridgewater. Mustachioed now, and with his hair down to his shoulders and his muscles bulging from years of karate practice at Matteawan and Manhattan State, Ricardo was something of an anomaly in the conventional little village. But Judith showed him around and then drove him to her family home. There, just as she had done with friends, she gave his name, but introduced him as a colleague. He worked at Manhattan State Hospital on Wards Island, she said.

Janie Becker remembered that afternoon. "He was charming," she told me in her cultivated, Connecticut voice. "More reserved than gregarious. And very self-confident."

Janie had liked him. "Over lunch, we talked about Argentina and his family. He told us his people were wealthy and that they'd sent him up here to study. I got the impression that he was quite intelligent. And sophisticated, something of a wine expert, especially when it came to Argentinian wines."

After lunch, Judith and Ricardo went swimming in the family pool. "You must have seen their picture at the pool," Janie said. "It was in all the newspapers."

I had. The picture showed Judith sitting in her two-piece bathing suit with her legs tightly crossed and her hands folded modestly in her lap, and

Ricardo grinning expansively and dangling his legs in the water. To me, he had looked like a man convinced that the sparkling pool at which he sat and the proper heiress who was perched beside him would one day surely be his.

"Were you at all worried about Ricardo that afternoon?" I asked Janie, hoping that she had been. I wanted to believe, will always want to believe, that the psychopath's disguise is porous, less impenetrable than textbooks tell us it is.

But, "Not at all," Janie said sadly. "He was no one you'd be suspicious of in any way."

That evening, Judith took a step toward extricating herself from her relationship with Ricardo. Instead of driving back to her apartment with him, as he expected her to do, she deposited him at a train station and stayed on in Connecticut. And soon she made another, more difficult move to disentangle herself from him. She terminated her pregnancy.

Around that time, she told Ricardo that she didn't want to see him anymore. In fact she had another boyfriend, she said, a police officer.

It was to no avail. Ricardo continued to call her and to drop in unannounced. And the more she tried to break up with him, the more possessive and furious he became. One day when he once again arrived unexpectedly at her apartment and she again made her wishes known, he shouted at her so angrily and loudly that some of her neighbors heard his rage through the walls.

Still, Judith stuck to her guns. And in the early autumn Ricardo seemed finally to accept her retreat, or at least to accept her insistence that he stop paying unannounced calls on her, for he ceased his visits. Judith was extremely relieved. "I feel," she told one of her closest friends, "like I have a monkey off my back."

But she hadn't reckoned on Ricardo's extraordinary ability to worm his way back into the good graces of those who wanted to be rid of him—or of those he deemed necessary to his future plans. And he had such plans. He was intending to escape from Manhattan State. One day he left the hospital and went to an antiques and used-clothing shop and there tried on a wig. Not long afterward he began withdrawing money from his bank account. He had almost six thousand dollars in it, money he would one day claim he had saved through the sale of his artwork and his job in the hospital cafeteria. He started by removing the money gradually. But on Friday, October 18, 1974, he closed the account altogether, taking out a final fifteen hundred dollars.

Judith was still refusing to see him, but she was allowing him to telephone her, and after closing his bank account, he called and spoke to her with a new, apologetic disarmingness. He was sorry he'd caused her pain, he said. And because he still loved her, he would absolutely and surely mend his irritable ways.

Judith must have judged him to be sincere, for she agreed to go out with him on Sunday. She even told her parents that she was going to do so—"my friend Ritchie is going to take me on a boat ride," she said.

But there was to be no boat ride. Ricardo, his money in the pocket of an expensive suit that Judith had bought for him in the heyday of their relationship, made his way to Yonkers and, after he arrived, said he didn't really want to go out, just wanted to hang around the apartment.

Judith let him stay and later in the day even agreed to make him dinner. Steak—his favorite. She

set two pretty plates down on her living-room cocktail table, put out a bottle of wine and two delicate-
stemmed glasses, and began broiling the meat. But
when it was done and they were eating it, Ricardo
began yelling at her. Perhaps he had just told her of
his plan to flee the hospital and she had attempted
to dissuade him. Or perhaps he had requested help
from her in the form of cash or her car and she had
refused. What he said to her or she to him cannot be
discovered. But whatever was said, Ricardo turned
belligerent and soon he was shouting at Judith so
vehemently that once again his voice pierced
through the walls of the apartment building.

A neighbor heard it. But she didn't think anything of it. She was used to the sounds of quarreling
coming from Judith's apartment.

But this time Ricardo didn't stop at shouting. He
pushed Judith into the bedroom, ripping off her
clothes until she had no covering but her panties.
He flung her onto the bed, but he didn't rape her.
Instead, he began pummeling her about the head,
breaking her nose and both her cheekbones. And
then, as blood poured down her face, he grabbed
one of the stockings he'd yanked off her and twisted
it tightly around her throat.

Next door, her neighbor heard sudden silence.
She didn't know that Judith had just died, that as
the stocking had tightened she had gasped one final
breath. Nor did the neighbor know that in the
silence she thought blessed, Ricardo was methodi-
cally cleaning himself up and riffling through
Judith's possessions in search of her wallet and car
keys.

A short while later Ricardo had found what he
wanted, and taking Judith's cash and car keys, he
went outside and looked for her car. It was parked
where she often left it, just behind her building. He

unlocked the door, started the car, and drove himself into Manhattan, where he abandoned the car near a bus terminal and boarded a bus headed to California.

Inside her apartment, Judith was still lying spread-eagled on the bed. Her face was completely awry, like a head begun by a sculptor who had changed his mind and mashed up his clay. Her neck was discolored, with a scar like a nightmare rainbow across it. And her eyes were open—wide open to Ricardo at last. She would remain just this way until the following afternoon when her parents, alarmed because she hadn't called them on Sunday night as was her wont, traveled to her apartment and let themselves in.

I knew only some of these facts at the time I interviewed Ann Berrill, one of Judith's high school friends who now practiced law. I'd found Ann by chance—she played in a women's poker group with a good friend of mine—and she'd agreed to meet me for brunch at a coffee shop near her apartment in midtown Manhattan.

"Why would a woman like Judith, a woman with professional training in psychology, fall in love with a Ricardo Caputo?" I began over our eggs and coffee.

"You have to remember where we came from," Ann said. "How sheltered we were."

"Of course."

"And you have to remember the era. It wasn't like today, after the AIDs scare, when people are cautious about who they get involved with. We got out of college, we started living on our own, and we went out with all sorts of creeps. Men we hardly knew anything about. It was pretty scary, let me tell you."

"It was the same for me when I got out of college.

God, when I think of some of the weirdos I went out with!"

"Exactly. Sometimes I wonder how any of us ever survived our young womanhood."

"You seem to have survived all right." I smiled.

"Yes. Sure. But you know, I chalk it up to luck. I mean, after Judith died, a lot of the women we'd known accused her of having had bad judgment. 'I'd never have gotten involved with a guy like that,' they said. Not me. Because a part of me always knew that in those days, if a fellow with the right line had come along, I'd have fallen for it."

I appreciated her candor and told her so, and Ann said, "Look, I think you're asking the wrong question. What you should ask is not why Judith fell for Ricardo, but how he made her fall. Some men have no skills at seduction. Some men know exactly how to go about it. How did Ricardo go about it?"

I told her about Ricardo's poetry—she hadn't known about it—and when I was done, Ann nodded and said, "Yes, that would have done it."

"Even though the poetry was kind of scary? I mean, in some of it he let her know outright about his moodiness, his jealousy."

"Yes, but he was writing. I know Judith. She'd have felt he was a wounded bird that she was nursing back to health."

Ann and I got on well, and a few weeks later, I met with her again because she'd offered to show me Judith's high school yearbook. This time we sat side by side in Ann's apartment, leafing through the yearbook and studying, first, the many pictures of New Milford High's class of 1966 at play or in their clubs. We saw Judith posing like a bookend back-to-back with a best friend, Judith lounging on a classroom floor with two other friends. Then we flipped to the part of the book that featured individual portraits of the graduates and their answers to the questions the yearbook editors had deemed important that year: What subjects had they failed? What were their pet peeves? What were their secret ambitions? There was Judith again, her smile gentle, the ends of her hair painstakingly flipped up in the most popular style of the period. And there were Judith's answers to the editors' questions.

When you write about murdered people, you frequently learn something that breaks your heart, some unexpected and often tiny detail. In Judith's case, it happened to me when I read the responses she'd given. I noted that she had failed gym, and that her pet peeves were naturally curly hair and having to wait for people. These replies were not very different from those of her fellow graduates. But her secret ambition was a world apart. Where her fellow graduates had responded with remarks like "To make a million dollars," "To own the *New York Times*," "To discover a cure for cancer," Judith had written, "To grow old gracefully."

6

I was still looking into Judith Becker's story when in November 1994, Nassau County's first hearing in the Caputo case got under way. I took the train out to Mineola, arriving in the midst of a dreadful downpour that was stripping the leaves from the trees around the courthouse and making the building's walkways into little rivers. But inside it was warm and dry, and I had no trouble getting a front-row seat—hardly anyone from the press was present. The media had been ignoring Caputo ever since June, when the O. J. Simpson case had broken.

Today's hearing was to be an investigation into whether Caputo's statements to the police at the time he killed Natalie had been legally and properly obtained. Lawrence Miron, the officer who had arrested Caputo, was to be examined in the matter. So was Bill Coningsby.

McCarthy was there, looking chic in a black suit and glistening pearls. Kennedy was there, too. I'd called his office, telling his secretary I was writing a book about Caputo and asking to speak to Kennedy, but she'd said he was no longer speaking to the press about the Caputo case. Later, still hoping that he might talk to me, and that if he did, he might be willing to put me in touch with Alberto and Kim Caputo, I'd written him a letter, reminding him that we'd met and requesting an interview. To prepare myself for the interview, I'd done a little research into his background. He'd started his career in the late 1960s and seemed then, and for many years afterward, primarily a political idealist. He'd defended radicals like Bernadine Dohrn and Black Panthers like Huey Newton. He'd been quoted as praising "almost any act that disrupts or disturbs the government" and predicted for America "a system where people work together in a Communist way." He'd also supported and become a spokesperson for left-wing movements like Nicaragua's Sandinistas. But in recent years he'd taken to defending extremely wealthy clients whose cases and causes were hardly the stuff of radical ideology—not just Ivana Trump, but even Gaetano Badalamenti, a heroin-dealing Mafia chieftan. Was he political or simply defiant? Did he act on the basis of ideas or self-interest?

I'd been eager to find out, to get more of a fix on him than I'd gotten when I'd met him socially. But Kennedy had replied to my letter with a note saying, "I am buried in trials now through May. Can we talk in June?" And when June had rolled around, although I'd called his office several times, his secretary hadn't put me through to him. Mr. Kennedy is too busy, she always said. He'll get back to you.

This morning, I found him impressive. After McCarthy took testimony from Officer Miron, Kennedy rose sternly to cross-examine him, and with virtually every question managed to imply that Caputo's English had been so bad at the time of Natalie's death that, absent a Spanish interpreter, his statements couldn't possibly be considered to have been properly obtained. "After you met him in the gas station," Kennedy said to Miron, "and after he said to you, 'I need help. I just killed Natalie,' you asked, 'Where?' Am I right? And then, when he didn't respond, your partner asked him the question in Spanish, right?"

"Yes," Miron said shortly. He was a hefty man in his mid-fifties who had left the police department years ago but still seemed imbued with the defiant brusqueness that many police officers manifest when they're questioned by defense attorneys. Kennedy wasn't fazed. "But back in 1971, the card that you police officers carry with the Miranda rights on them didn't yet have them written in Spanish," he continued, one hand in his pants pocket, as if to prevent it from moving, the other gesticulating rhythmically to the beat of his words. "Am I right?"

"Yes," Miron said again.

"Did it occur to you when you read Caputo his rights that he might need a Spanish translation of them?"

"No."

"And when you turned him over to Detective Coningsby, did you say anything to the detective about Caputo's ability to understand English?" Kennedy's unpocketed hand was dancing and his deep voice had grown louder.

"No."

"Were you present when Coningsby interrogated him?"

"Yes."

"And you say that Caputo initialed each page of the statement and read it aloud?"

"Yes."

Kennedy leaned forward on the podium, both hands still now. "How? Was his English fluent? Or hesitant?"

Miron leaned forward, too. "It was fine. When he read the statement back to me, I understood what he was reading."

Kennedy grimaced broadly. And a few moments later, he announced he was finished with Miron.

Coningsby took the stand next. Under McCarthy's questioning, the suntanned detective, who'd flown in that morning from South Carolina, described the crime scene and related the contents of Caputo's confession statement. Coningsby also mentioned that after the statement was written out, an assistant district attorney had arrived and interrogated Caputo further. But he didn't have a copy of that interrogation. "There was a fire in the warehouse where a lot of our records were stored," he explained. "We think the Q and A burned up."

I wondered what Kennedy would have to say about that, but he didn't get a chance to cross-examine Coningsby. The judge announced it was time for lunch.

The area around most courthouses, except in Manhattan where the courts are cheek by jowl with Chinatown, is a culinary wasteland. So I didn't expect to find a decent restaurant. I just left the building, ran through the cold, still-pelting rain, and entered the first eatery I encountered. It was an Asian lunch counter where the food, precooked and displayed in warming trays, looked gluey and unidentifiable. I ordered something the counterman said was chicken and vegetables and started to put it down on a table, when suddenly I noticed Kennedy behind me. He, too, had chosen this closest-at-hand canteen.

What good fortune! I suggested we eat together. "Maybe we could do that interview about your past," I said.

"My past? I don't think I want to talk about that over lunch," he frowned. "It might make me sick."

"Maybe," I laughed, "we can find other things to talk about."

"Sure."

He slid opposite me into the booth, and we began talking. I didn't bring up Kennedy's past—I knew the ground rules. But I told him a little about mine, specifically that I'd known Jacqui Bernard. "Her brother-in-law is a good friend," Kennedy said. "He called me up right after the story appeared in the newspaper and I told him I didn't think Caputo had killed Jacqui." Kennedy also mentioned that he'd spoken to a Manhattan Homicide investigator about Jacqui. "I told him," he said, "that Caputo was living in L.A. at the time Jacqui was murdered." I nodded when he said that—it was pretty much what Detective Giorgio had told me Kennedy had said to him, which was that Caputo had been living in L.A. and that he categorically denied having had any-thing to do with Jacqui's death. The denial hadn't meant much to me. As a judge friend of mine likes to say, "If a man can kill, he can lie."

Still, I didn't want to get off on the wrong foot with Kennedy. So I let it go, returning to the subject of Jacqui's brother-in-law, whom I also knew, and chatting about him and about our other mutual friends, the couple who'd once taken me to that party at Kennedy's house. Small talk. And then after a while Kennedy brought up Ricardo again. I guess his client was too much on his mind for him to avoid talking about him altogether. "You know, I told Ricardo on the phone the first time I spoke to him that there was no way he was going to see the light of day. He'd either go to a prison or a mental hospital for life."

I wanted to ask, you mean he turned himself in

even after knowing you—his lawyer—thought this? Why would someone do that? But before I could get the words out of my mouth, Kennedy started telling me that Caputo could have turned himself in to either New York or California, but had selected New York. And then, as if in answer to the unspoken questions that had earlier crossed my mind, he said, "I don't ask Caputo much, because he's wacky. He's so wacky I can't believe the things he says."

I didn't think Caputo was wacky. It was hard to think this now that I'd learned how he'd rallied himself after killing Natalie Brown and how carefully he'd planned his escape from Manhattan State Hospital just before he killed Judith Becker. Wacky people are seldom capable of such organization.

Kennedy must have seen the skepticism in my face. "Just to show you how wacky Caputo was," he said, "he left clues behind at all his killings. Here in Nassau, he left his watch and his shoes and socks."

"But he changed his clothes," I pointed out. "Threw his shirt into a trash can. I found that an important detail."

Kennedy didn't think so. But of course it was, suggesting as it did that Caputo had had at least some awareness of the difference between right and wrong when he killed Natalie, and Kennedy, for all his denial, appeared to be listening to me carefully. Maybe he's wondering how he'll explain away that discarded shirt, I thought. Not today. It wasn't relevant to the hearing. But it might be a different story in front of a jury.

Then Kennedy mentioned something that he did seem to find significant. "That Q and A that disappeared," he said. And he added, with a twinkle in his eyes, "An unscrupulous lawyer could make a lot out of that."

Not long afterward, the lawyer cut our conversation short, saying he had to get back to the court-house. I was disappointed. I hadn't even gotten around to asking him if he'd put me in touch with Alberto and Kim Caputo. But he was out the door already. I put on my raincoat and sloshed my way back to the courtroom.

There, that afternoon, Kennedy cross-examined Coningsby. But although he raised the matter of the vanished Q and A, he didn't dwell on it. Nor did he go back to the question of why the police hadn't pro-vided Caputo with a Spanish interpreter. Indeed, he seemed distracted, as if his mind was no longer fully on the hearing, and as soon as it ended, he raced out of the building.

"What did you think of Kennedy's cross-exami-nation?" Elise McCarthy asked me over the phone several days later.

"It was okay," I said noncommittally.

"Well, I thought it was terrible. I thought he seemed nervous." McCarthy was fierce, a young Turk battling the hegemony of the old. She was also unusually voluble. "Kennedy and I had something of a dustup," she said. "Before the hearing started, we went in back and he said to me, 'If Dr. Dietz finds Caputo not responsible, you're not going to dispute it, are you?' And I said, 'It depends what Dietz bases his conclusions on. I mean, have you guys done an investigation of how Caputo's spent the past twenty years?' Kennedy didn't answer that. He just said, 'The defendant's told Dietz everything.' So I said, 'Well, we've done an investigation.' So then he want-ed to know if he had everything I had, and I said, 'Do your own investigation!' And he stormed out."

I scribbled furiously, relishing her loquacious account but wishing she'd slow down so I could uncramp my fingers.

But McCarthy kept talking. "And that wasn't the end of it. During the lunch break, he brought it up again. He said, 'Look, I really don't want to go through all this. I'm really just going through the motions here. This isn't going to be a trial, is it?' And then he went, 'What if Dietz doesn't say Caputo's not responsible, but he says it was extreme emotional distress? What then? Would you consider a manslaughter plea?' "

"Would you?" I managed to interrupt.

Her answer was indirect. "What I *thought* was, Frankly, I'd take that in a second. But I couldn't believe Kennedy was really saying he wanted it. I mean, if Caputo took a manslaughter plea here in Nassau, it'd be hard for him to go ahead and argue insanity in any of the other jurisdictions."

Despite my aching fingers, I was delighted to receive this behind-the-scenes account, which went a long way toward explaining why Kennedy had seemed so effective the morning of the hearing and so desultory in the afternoon. He talks to McCarthy after our Asian lunch, I speculated, he figures she's going to go for the manslaughter deal, and so he lets himself just peddle down.

But if McCarthy *was* going to go for a manslaughter plea, she wasn't telling me. When I asked her directly if such a plea was now in the works, she stopped talking.

I didn't want to end our conversation on that silence, so I said, "By the way, how *did* Caputo spend the last twenty years?"

"Well, there's a lot I can't tell you just yet," McCarthy said, her speed down to normal now. "But there's more to this guy's history than he's admitting to."

"Like what?"

"Like an *attempted* murder, maybe. Talk to

Sanders about it." Sanders was the detective in San Francisco who'd investigated Caputo's third admitted murder, that of Barbara Taylor. I'd mentioned to McCarthy that I was going out to the Coast shortly to interview him about Taylor.

"I will," I promised. "I sure will."

7

Taylor, a documentary filmmaker and the director of a McGraw-Hill subsidiary called Contemporary Films, had been twenty-eight years old when she was killed. Caputo had not yet been arraigned for her murder and all press inquiries were being handled not by San Francisco's district attorney's office but by its police department, and specifically by Inspector Earl Sanders. He was an authority on the nature and apprehension of serial killers. And he had a special interest in the Caputo case, having been one of the first detectives to discover Barbara Taylor's body.

I'd talked to Sanders on the phone several times, told him about how I'd gotten interested in Caputo, filled him in on how the Nassau and Westchester cases were proceeding, and then made our interview date. I was to fly to San Francisco, and he was to pick me up in front of Nordstrom's and take me to police headquarters.

I'm always apprehensive before an interview. Partly, it's the remnant of my old shyness, but partly it's because conducting an interview is not unlike giving a performance. You have lines—the questions you've meticulously prepared and rehearsed.

You have a costume—you don't wear your everyday writing clothes, your baggy jeans and shapeless T-shirts, but something tailored and chic and responsible-looking. And you have stage fright, a turbulence in the pit of your stomach. Maybe the interviewee won't respond to you, you tell yourself, won't open up, won't give you the information you so long to obtain.

These customary anxieties multiplied as I waited for Sanders in front of Nordstrom's for he was nowhere in evidence. He's probably just late, I tried to reassure myself. He'll be here any minute. But as I lingered on that unfamiliar, crowded street corner, I grew more and more uncomfortable. And then Sanders, a portly man dressed in a black trench coat and a black fedora with a jaunty red feather in its band, pulled up in a green Jeep Cherokee and waved to me. He recognized me. He'd seen my picture on a book jacket, he told me. And I recognized him. I'd seen him on the TV show *America's Most Wanted*, and although the show had been taped a few years ago and he was heavier now, he had the same sparkling eyes and genial expression.

By the time we neared police headquarters in a run-down, warehouse-laden section of San Francisco, I had relaxed, for it was impossible in Sanders's company to feel anything but at ease. He was a talker, a man who liked sharing the pungent anecdotes of the policeman's life. "I had this case once," he said as he drove, "where this guy murdered his mother and got off. End of story? Hell, no. Mom's dead, he's got no one to hate, he goes and shoots his lawyer." And, "I had this teenager we call the Kervorkian kid. Him and another kid twisted a rope around a girl's neck, and they each held an end and gave it a yank. End of story? No, the kid says, 'The girl wanted to die, and she asked for our help.

It ain't murder if you're just lending a hand to a friend who wants to kill herself.' "

Sanders was just as voluble once we reached the headquarters, where he made us a pot of coffee, plunked himself and a stack of thick loose-leaf notebooks opposite me at a beaten-up desk, and saying he didn't hold with the kind of police paranoia that insisted on secrecy even where none was necessary, as in this ancient Taylor case, proceeded to tell me everything he knew about it. "Barbara was a terrific person," he began, leafing through one of the notebooks. "She had loads of friends, and every one of them described her as someone they loved and trusted and liked to be around. Here. This is typical. One of her friends told us, 'If people needed assistance, Barbara was always there.' "

"A nurturer?" I asked, thinking of Jacqui Bernard.

"Exactly."

"What did she look like?"

Sanders flipped to another document and started to read me a description of her. "Well, she was five feet eight inches tall, weighed a hundred and fifty-five pounds, had brown hair and eyes—but wait. You might as well see for yourself." At this he handed me a collection of photographs of Barbara, who was attractive not in a glamorous but in a completely artless way. Her long, dark hair hung loosely to her shoulders, her large, unpainted eyes were luminous, and her unglossed lips stretched wide into an infectious smile.

"What did she do at Contemporary Films?" I asked.

"She managed the U.S. distribution of educational documentaries. Traveled abroad to acquire foreign productions. Made good money."

Barbara's salary, I soon learned, had allowed her

to take an apartment in Pacific Heights, one of San Francisco's loveliest neighborhoods, a hilly tumble of fretted Victorian houses, elaborate stone mansions from the twenties, and graceful, low pre–World War II apartment buildings, set on steep streets with spectacular views of the Bay. "Ricardo Caputo liked the neighborhood," Sanders sniffed. "Before he met Barbara, he was living in a flophouse off Broadway."

He was in San Francisco because after the long cross-country bus ride he'd embarked on the night he killed Judith, he'd decided to make his new home there. Back in New York, he was the subject of public outrage. Newspaper editorials were denouncing government officials for putting people like him into minimum-security hospitals and attacking the administrators of those hospitals for letting patients elope. But in San Francisco, a city thronged with tourists and the itinerant peddlers who made their living off them, he apparently felt safe. He shaved off his mustache, cut his hair, obtained a new identity from a dealer in black-market documents, and began going out in public, drawing penciled portraits in the heavily trafficked bars and cafés of North Beach and Union Street.

"I don't think he intended to make a living as a portrait artist," Sanders told me dryly. "No, he's a guy who loves the feeding trough. He was looking for something more lucrative, for someone who'd support him."

He found that someone in Barbara Taylor, just a month after he killed Judith. One night after work, Barbara strolled the two blocks between her apartment and Union Street and ended her walk by going into Moonie's, an Irish bar and café frequented by young professionals like herself. Ricardo was drawing there, and she stopped to look at his work.

When she did, he offered to sketch her, and when she said okay, he began talking to her. He said his name was Ricardo Donoguier, and that he was from Argentina, where his family owned a big ranch. He said he'd be inheriting the ranch one day, but that in the meantime, he preferred the joys of expressing himself creatively. And he said that he supplemented his income as an artist by working as a waiter or busboy and was looking for such a position just now.

Barbara was intrigued by him. She bought his portrait of her. And she took another picture as well, a drawing of Humphrey Bogart. It wasn't very good. Bogart's face looked pinched and elongated. But Barbara thought both drawings showed talent. And later that night, after talking some more with Ricardo, she invited him to come home with her.

"It was that kind of time," Sanders said. "Women were moving, making their stand, doing things they'd never done before. We don't know whether Barbara was in the habit of inviting men home with her right after she met them, but she did it with Ricardo. We do know that she'd never *lived* with a man before, and yet pretty much right after that first night, she started living with Ricardo. That is, he started living with her. Brought his things over and moved right in."

Sanders had talked to a great many of Barbara's friends and gotten pretty much the same story from all of them: that she said she'd met the most wonderful man at Moonie's; that she said she was having with him the most incredible relationship; and that she didn't keep her new boyfriend hidden. "She showed him off," Sanders said. "Brought him to her office. Went out to dinner in little ethnic restaurants with him. She also spent money on him. Paid for those dinners. Gave him carfare and a small lunch

allowance so he could go out job hunting. Bought
him clothing. He liked good stuff, and she got it for
him. Fancy sneakers. Even a pair of expensive suede
hiking boots with steel-reinforced heels."

She bought him the boots so that they could go
hiking at Yosemite and, when they went, did what
Natalie had done when she and Ricardo traveled to
the Caribbean—paid for the trip. Barbara took a
thousand dollars out of her bank account and supplemented the cash by using her credit card, too.
She also, during their stay in the majestic park,
snapped picture after picture of Ricardo, although
when they returned home she neglected to get the
pictures developed.

"We found the roll in her apartment after he
killed her," Sanders said to me. "Wanna see?" And
he laid out in front of me a handful of snapshots of
Ricardo. In one, he was bare-armed and bare-chest-
ed, his muscles visible under his well-tanned skin.
In another, he was perched in a tree, balancing himself proudly on its precarious branches. In all the
pictures, he was smiling—a lighthearted, confident
smile.

"Yeah, she was enthralled by him," Sanders said
as, struck most of all by that smile, I studied the pictures. Ricardo didn't look like a man who had a care
in the world, let alone a man who had murdered
two women.

"He was like a beautiful snake," Sanders murmured. "He got Barbara so enthralled that she forgot that beautiful snakes can have deadly venom." A
moment later, Sanders took the pictures back and,
staring at them himself, added, "No, he was more
like a leech. He lived off women, that was his game.
And he could be quite expensive."

"Could Barbara afford him?" I asked, a part of
me wanting the pictures back, imagining that if I

studied those smiling images long enough, I might, after all, see some hint of Ricardo's true nature. I'd have felt more secure in the world if I could have detected that. But Sanders was putting the photographs away.

"Well, she wasn't rich," he answered my question. "Her family was middle class. Her father was a high school principal in Union City. She didn't have money, just her salary. And a bit of savings. But Ricardo, he was determined to get his hands on every last bit of it."

According to Sanders, this became clear to Barbara when, sometime after the trip to Yosemite, Ricardo began hitting her up not just for lunches, dinners, and local trips, but for something more costly—a trip to Hawaii. Barbara resented the demand and said so to several friends. But if she had begun to suspect that Ricardo was interested in her not for herself but for her money, she had also begun to feel, whether for this reason or another, that she herself was no longer interested in him. After a while, she gave in to his demand for plane fare to Hawaii and told one intimate, "I want to be rid of him. I bought him a one-way ticket."

"End of story?" Sanders said. "No. Ricardo was out of her hair, but not for long. He went out to Hawaii. Tried to pick up women. Looked for a place to stay. Knocked on the door of some painter and told her he'd been given her name by someone in San Francisco. This woman didn't know anyone in San Francisco. But she let Ricardo spend the night at her place anyway—that's how ingratiating he could be. Still, she didn't let him stay longer than just that one night. He didn't find a meal ticket. Not like Barbara. So just before Christmas, he phoned her and begged her for a return air ticket. He missed her, he said, and wanted to spend the holiday with her."

Barbara had been planning to spend it with her parents and sister. But she bought him a ticket. And on Christmas Day, she brought him with her to the family gathering, just as Judith Becker had brought him to *her* family's gathering. And just as he had done with Judith Becker's family, and with that of Natalie Brown, he made a favorable impression, mingling sociably and talking interestingly about his life in Argentina. Indeed, Judson and Vera Taylor, Barbara's father and mother, thought him a most sincere and serious young man, and Barbara's sister, Susan, decided he was deeply in love with Barbara.

But Barbara knew better. And after Christmas, when Ricardo asked her for more money, she coolly refused him.

"We know this for a fact," Sanders said, and shoved a piece of paper at me. It was a police department interview with a dealer in guns and false identity papers who had been visited by Ricardo shortly before New Year's Day. "Ricardo had a big powerful gun that he wanted to sell," the detective who had written up the interview reported. "Ricardo said that Barbara took care of him . . . [but] he was going to drop her because she wasn't giving him enough money. Ricardo told the dealer to tell him of a place with a lot of money. He wanted to rob the place. . . . He said he'd [already] 'knocked down' two places. The gun that Ricardo wanted to sell was a handmade gun, chrome-plated, with a pearl handle. . . . Ricardo said he'd asked Barbara for a lot of money—like $1,000—and she'd refused. He was upset about that."

I'd known that Ricardo had had some experience with theft. After all, Detective Pierce, to whom I'd spoken in connection with the murder of Natalie Brown, had told me that a man who'd roomed with

Ricardo when he first came to the States had claimed to the police that Ricardo used to rough up and rob gay men. That knowledge had several times made me wonder about the source of the money Ricardo had had in the bank just before he murdered Judith Becker. Six thousand dollars. Surely that was a far more substantial sum than an inmate might have been expected to earn from working in the hospital cafeteria and selling an occasional pencil sketch. But even with my suspicions about how he came by money, here was a Ricardo Caputo I hadn't expected. Here was a Ricardo Caputo with clear-cut underworld aspirations and contacts, with the kinds of ambitions and friends that would surely have startled the dutiful daughters and hardworking professional women whom he courted.

I shook my head, and Sanders read my expression. "You know, people think Ricardo Caputo was just a lady-killer," he said. "Some kind of romantic with a screw loose. But the fact of the matter is that killing women was just the tip of his iceberg. You'll see as we move along that he was a thug, a guy whose chief interest was money and who knew how to get it in a lot of different ways. Most of them outside the law."

We'd been talking a long time, and at this juncture Sanders got up and poured us both some more coffee. "We are going to move along, aren't we?" he said as he did so. "I've got lots more to tell. You got the time?"

Was he serious? I'd been mesmerized by his information, so mesmerized that I'd forgotten to bring up the attempted murder that McCarthy had suggested I ask him about. As soon as our cups were full and he had seated himself again, I did so, interrupting his account of Barbara. "Elise McCarthy in

Nassau mentioned another case to me. An attempted murder. Was it here? In San Francisco?"

"Ah, you know about that?"

I nodded as if I did, or at least as if I knew more than just what I'd said. And Sanders started talking again. "It was in Hawaii. After that meeting with the gun dealer, Ricardo hightailed it back there."

"Because Barbara wouldn't give him any more money?"

"Maybe. But probably not. Maybe it was just because by this time, he'd hooked up with a man who made his living by stealing credit card numbers and using them to purchase and then sell expensive goods. Ricardo was a good sidekick for this guy. He knew how to be a waiter, and waiters knew how to get their hands on credit card numbers."

Ricardo's new friend had an attractive two-bedroom apartment in one of Waikiki Beach's most pleasant neighborhoods, an area of small apartment buildings built before the trend to mammoth high-rises, and one that was just a few blocks from the water. He offered Ricardo a room in his place, and Ricardo got himself a waiter's job at a popular restaurant.

Ricardo remained in the apartment for several months, enjoying a life that was very much to his taste. He only worked lunches, and when his labors were over, he donned a pair of minuscule bathing trunks, sunned his muscular body at the beach, then wandered the sands hoping to pick up tourists and shake them down for cash or meals. "He had quite a system," Sanders said. "He'd start by offering to take the tourists out. Then he'd get them to take *him* out. We know this because of what happened next. With the woman you asked me about. Her name was Mary O'Neill. He met her late in March and invited her out to dinner and she went."

"Just like that?"

"Yeah, well, he told her he owned a restaurant—the one he worked in. Oh, he could shovel it, he could shovel it with the best of them. O'Neill was impressed, and she goes out for a steak dinner with him. Then he asks her to buy *him* dinner the next night, but she can't, she's going on a tour of the island. End of story? No. The next day, he finds her and tells her he knows a little beach that's better than anything she's seen on her tour and he'll take her there. Maybe he only has her wallet on his mind, but then he gets another idea, tells her they have to stop at his apartment first because he needs something."

I gave a little groan. I could see what was coming.

"Yeah," Sanders said. "But I go back to my snake analogy. He had so much charm that O'Neill trusted him, forgot about poison. She says yes, she'll go with him. They get to his apartment. He hits on her, starts kissing and petting her. She goes along with it for a while. But then she wants him to stop. And he won't stop. He starts to rape her. She resists. And he begins beating her. Hard. And then all of a sudden, his roommate comes home, shouts at Ricardo to stop, and O'Neill gets away and runs screaming out of the apartment."

"Lucky woman," I sighed. "I mean, suppose the roommate hadn't come home."

"Exactly. Exactly. But hold on, there's something I want to show you. Because it's going to help you understand Barbara Taylor better." He began rummaging in one of his notebooks, then snapped out a sheet of paper.

"Mary O'Neill didn't report the attack to the police," Sanders said. "But Ricardo figured she would, and pronto, he moved out. And then, incredibly, the next day she went looking for him and left this with his roommate." Shaking his head, he handed me the piece of paper.

It was a letter that Mary O'Neill had written to Ricardo, and I saw at once why Sanders had wanted me to read it. Its few short lines conveyed better than all his words that Ricardo did indeed possess an extraordinary ability to fascinate women—and to hold on to them even after they had become acquainted with his viciousness.

"Dear Ricardo," O'Neill had written. "I can't believe that you would do something like this to me. Your roommate said you don't live here anymore. I feel very bad about all this. Maybe you could at least write to me and tell me what changed *please!*"

The note was plaintive, but what was most telling about it was its end. Despite having been beaten by Ricardo, despite having escaped his violence merely by the timely return of his roommate, O'Neill wanted to hear from him again. She finished her missive by giving Ricardo her home address in upstate New York.

I was stunned by this example of Ricardo's capacity to enthrall, so stunned that I asked if I might copy it out then and there. Sanders said yes, and I began to write. And maybe it was because Sanders saw me sitting there studentlike and quietly scribbling away, but as I wrote, he turned professorial. "You know, it isn't just Ricardo. A lot of serial killers have this uncanny ability to get women—yeah, and men, too—to put themselves in harm's way. You know, we know a lot about them. Even that they've been around for centuries. Probably inspired all those stories about werewolves."

"But *is* Caputo a serial killer?" I asked, handing him back Mary O'Neill's letter. "From what I've read, they kill for the thrill of killing, while he seems to kill because women reject him or some demand of his. At least, that's what seems to have happened with the first two women. And what almost happened with O'Neill."

"Well, I'll tell you this. Caputo's a little different from your garden-variety serial killer, but yes, I'd term him a serial killer. He's different in that he got into relationships with his victims—at least, with the victims whose murders he's confessed. But he may have killed a lot more people. Remember, Gordon McEwan's informant said he bragged about having killed men as well as women. And even as far as women go, I'm sure he's killed more than those four he's taking the credit for. You know about the one in L.A.?"

"A little."

Sanders fisted a hand, then raised a thumb. "Okay. In 1981, four years after Caputo claims to have stopped killing, a woman who works with him at a restaurant in L.A.—her name is Devon Green— is found murdered." He raised his index finger. "Okay. They find her body and Caputo isn't questioned because he isn't known to have any relationship with the woman." He raised his middle finger. "But hell, Caputo was married at the time. Maybe he was seeing her on the sly and asked her to keep it quiet."

I sat forward. "Maybe it was the same with Jacqui Bernard. She didn't tell anyone about Ricardo, and maybe it was because *he* asked her not to."

"Maybe. The funny thing is, we can't find the wife. She disappeared."

"You mean the one that was on *PrimeTime*?"

"No. That was his second wife. I'm talking about the first one. A Cuban refugee he says he married in 1979 and split up with in 1984. Name's Felicia Fernandez. We can't find her anywhere. Her or the two children he says he had with her. Maybe she ran away because she wanted to make sure *he* never found her. Or maybe he killed her, too. But whatever, back in 1983, when your friend was murdered—"

"He was still married to Felicia?"

"Right. And working in L.A. But the wife's gone, so we don't know if he was always at home. And maybe he wasn't *always* at work. Who's to say he didn't go East for a while?"

I nodded. I'd thought that ever since Kennedy had told me that Caputo couldn't have killed Jacqui because he was living in L.A. when she was murdered.

"Look, I'll tell you something else," Sanders interrupted my thoughts. "If Ricardo Caputo told me he'd stopped killing after murdering just four women, I'd tell him to his face, you're a liar. I'd tell him, the only reason you're not copping to any other murders is because you know which are the ones we've got the goods on you for—the ones where we know you were involved with the victims. But that doesn't mean you didn't do any more. Because serial killers don't stop killing. They can't."

My thoughts were racing, my mind on Jacqui. *Had* Gordon McEwan's informant been right? Had Caputo murdered her? So much that I'd learned today suggested its likelihood. But we went back to Barbara Taylor, and Sanders told me the end of her story.

The day after the O'Neill incident, Barbara was at her job at the film company when she received a call from Ricardo. He had fled Hawaii right after Mary O'Neill had run from his apartment, had flown all night, and was now in the San Francisco airport. He'd come home, Ricardo said to Taylor, because he'd realized he loved her and wanted to marry her.

And would she please come and pick him up at the airport.

She went, though she had no intention of resuming her relationship with Ricardo. Deflecting his protestations of love but agreeing to pick him up and let him rest at her apartment until her workday was finished, she left her office, fetched him, dropped him off at the apartment, and went back to work. But when she got to her desk, she called a man with whom she had made a date for the evening, broke the date, and explained that she couldn't keep it because her old boyfriend had turned up unexpectedly and she had to go home and get him to understand once and for all that they were through.

That evening she did just that. Did it firmly and directly. Ricardo exploded. He acted "as if I owed him something," she confided to a friend the next morning. But he was gone, and she felt safe. So that day, Good Friday, she relaxed, shopping for groceries at a local market and treating herself to coffee at an Italian coffeehouse. She lingered a long time over the coffee, sitting alone at a marble-topped table. Then eventually she went home.

There was no sign of Ricardo, who seemed to have accepted her wishes and gone his own way. But the following night one of her neighbors was awakened by the sound of a man and woman quarreling and shouting at each other. The neighbor didn't call the police, just burrowed his head down into his pillow. And while he tried to get back to sleep, Ricardo began beating Barbara Taylor, just as he'd beaten Mary O'Neill. This time, however, no door opened, no rescuing roommate returned. Ricardo socked Barbara in the face with one of his iron fists, splitting her skin just above the eyelid. Then he punched her in the eye. Then he knocked her to the ground.

Barbara was naked, but he didn't rape her. He just began kicking her, forcing his booted feet into her soft flesh. He struck a thigh, an arm, a hand. Then he began concentrating on her head, crashing his boot into her ear, her forehead, the back of her skull. He rammed into these places so hard that he split the skin right down to the bone.

Punching and kicking at her, he kept up his onslaught for an agonizingly long time—nearly fifteen minutes, the police were to estimate. But at last she was dead, as dead as she'd have been if he'd used a gun or a knife instead of his hands and feet. When he realized it, he threw a towel over her bleeding head, as if to make her face go away. But he could still see her body, the body he had so often made love to, and snatching an electric blanket from the bed, he draped it over her, so that at last she was covered, invisible to him. Then he scurried through the apartment, searched the drawers and closets for money, and hurriedly disappeared into the now silent night.

"I didn't know about it until the next day," Sanders said when he'd finished describing the murder to me. "Easter Sunday. Barbara's father had gone to her apartment because she hadn't shown up for the family's Easter dinner, and he discovered the body and phoned the police. My partner and I were on call that day. We went over, saw the body, looked for the murder weapon. But we couldn't find one. Then we started looking harder, digging into the bottoms of drawers and the backs of closets. And way in the back of one closet, we found a suede boot covered with blood. It was the murder weapon. One of those pretty boots Barbara had bought Ricardo."

8

When I got back to New York, my mind was ablaze with the new information I'd learned. Mary O'Neill. Devon Green. These were new names to me, an example, in O'Neill's case, of how charming the canny Ricardo could be, and in Green's case, of the possibility that he was lying about the number of murders he had committed. I called Elise McCarthy to tell her what I'd learned from Sanders and to see if I could get more information about O'Neill and Green from her.

I was in luck, at least about O'Neill. McCarthy had just been to see her. "I needed to because, as I told you, if Kennedy goes ahead with the insanity defense, it isn't just Natalie's killing that's relevant, but everything Caputo's done *since* he killed her. So O'Neill becomes very important."

"Where does she live? Where did you see her?"

"I can't tell you that. She doesn't want to talk to a journalist. She didn't even want to talk to me."

"Why not?"

"Because she's scared out of her mind, that's why. Ever since the news about Barbara Taylor broke and she realized that the guy who'd beaten her in Hawaii was the same guy who killed Taylor, she's been looking over her shoulder, afraid that he might come back and get her."

I was relieved to hear that O'Neill, after writing her plaintive missive to Ricardo, had come to her senses about him. But I was frustrated, too. Here was a living victim of Caputo's and I wasn't going to get to speak to her. Not that I needed McCarthy to tell me how to find her. I could have done it on my own, using her old address as a way of tracing her. But I knew I wasn't going to do that. I was going to respect her terror, and McCarthy's obvious wish that I do so.

Still, I longed to know more about O'Neill. And one day, during an interview with a Nassau County detective, Robert Hines, my longing bore fruit. Hines was putting together a dossier for McCarthy on Caputo's activities since 1971. A chunky, broad-faced man with short-cropped, graying hair, he resembled Hollywood's version of the hard-as-nails Southern sheriff. But Hines wasn't ignorant and explosive like those celluloid sheriffs. He was smart, measured, observant. Indeed, he had a gaze so intent that at times I felt he wasn't just studying me but memorizing me. Despite this, however, I found him a pleasure to talk to, for unlike Sanders, he had actually met with and spoken to Ricardo, albeit briefly, on the night he had turned himself in.

"Ya ever notice his hands?" Hines asked me.

"Not that I can remember."

"They've got calluses on them. And the calluses are in a funny place. Most people get calluses on their palms. He's got them on the front of his hands. Ya know why?"

I shook my head.

"From doing push-ups. On his knuckles. I saw that as soon as I met him. Made me suspicious of him."

Hines had noticed other small but significant things about Ricardo, the kinds of details that only a man skilled at detection would not just observe but find useful. He'd seen, for example, a tiny scar on Ricardo's arm and been able to postulate that despite Ricardo's claims to insanity, he'd made a very sane effort to disguise his identity, for the scar turned out to be the result of the removal of a tattoo. Hines, whose eyes were never altogether still, seemed to rely a great deal on visual clues, on what he could learn from telltale revelations on skin, and from faces, whether seen in the flesh or in photographs. He was a Sherlock Holmes in a gray suit, white shirt, and paisley tie.

I was talking to him at Nassau County Police Headquarters, sitting opposite him at a big table in a deserted hearing room. On the table was a storage box, one of those cardboard boxes that is used to transport files. I kept glancing at it, wondering what it contained. And then Hines began pulling out its treasures. Photographs of Natalie Brown. Photographs of her parents' home. Photographs of Ricardo. In one, he was sitting on a low stone wall with a glorious blue sea behind him.

"You wanted to know about O'Neill?" Hines said, pushing the picture closer to me. "Well, I got this picture of Ricardo in Hawaii from her. She kept it all these years. Kept it because once she knew what the guy she'd met in Hawaii was capable of, she wanted always to be able to remember what he looked like. In case he turned up at her house."

"What's she like?"

"Married. Got a couple of kids. Nice lady."

Hines had located her through her old address and gone to visit her, but she'd been less than forthcoming on his visit. "My showing up scared her. After Taylor was killed, she'd been contacted by a

San Francisco detective who'd gotten her address off a note she left for Ricardo. That had weirded her out, made her worry that Ricardo might reach out and hurt her or her family. So she'd moved, changed her name, tried to disappear. But then, when Caputo's name surfaced in connection with the Jacqui Bernard killing, some New York City detectives managed to locate her. And now, here I was. And if I could find her, Ricardo could." Hines stared at the picture. "Ya see the smile?"

I did. Ricardo looked as cheerful as he'd looked in the pictures Barbara Taylor had taken of him in Yosemite.

"I had to reassure O'Neill that Ricardo was in jail," Hines went on. "But even so, she didn't want to talk to me. Like I said, she was frightened. But there was more. She didn't want to have this old stuff dredged up. She made it clear that what had happened to her with Ricardo had, in a way, happened to another woman. The woman she was twenty years ago. A tourist on a vacation."

Poor O'Neill, I thought. She'd gone off on a holiday, had a little fling, and then been haunted by it the rest of her life. I was glad I'd decided not to try to find her.

"So I left," Hines was saying. "What else could I do? But I must have won her confidence, because after I left, she sent me the picture. So I went back. I took Elise McCarthy with me. We drove up there—upstate New York, to hell and gone, and the whole time Elise was complaining about my driving. Too fast for her." He smiled at the idea of his speed having worried a presumably intrepid assistant district attorney. "But it was still no go. We sat at O'Neill's kitchen table and begged her to say she'd testify against Caputo if we needed her to. We practically went down on our hands and knees. But she was adamant, and we left without getting a commitment from her."

I had told Hines I wanted to know as much as he could tell me about Ricardo's past, and now he produced from his storage box a time chart he had made, two big sheets of taped-together cardboard covered with bold, hand-drawn lines and inky scrawls. The lines were for years. The scrawls were for the names of the women Caputo had admitted killing, the names of the women he was suspected of having killed, and the names of the cities and towns all across America where, with painstaking effort, Hines was gradually establishing that Caputo had on occasion been present.

One of them was El Paso, Texas. Four days after killing Barbara Taylor, Caputo had turned up at a bridge that spans the Rio Grande between El Paso and Juarez, Mexico, and attempted, without documents, to talk his way across the border. He had said first that he was a Mexican returning home. But when Mexican border guards heard him talk, they had become suspicious of his accent, and he had backtracked, admitted he was from South America. He'd been a stowaway, he said, and had just gotten off an Argentinian ship that had docked in Florida.

The Mexican guards turned him over to U.S. authorities, who placed him in an El Paso detention camp. There, he was fingerprinted and interviewed by two FBI agents, and he might have been caught except for two things—the slowness with which fingerprints could be compared in those mid-1970s, precomputer days, and his own astonishing quickness. Having learned by the time of the interview an arcane piece of information, which was that while stowaways fell under the jurisdiction of the FBI, deserters from their country's ships did not, he amended his story and claimed to be not a stowaway but a defector. As a result, the FBI agents had no choice but to turn him over to Immigration investigators. Of course, those investigators also attempted to interview him, but Ricardo had learned something else as well, had discovered that he needn't talk to Immigration without being represented by an attorney. So, demanding time to get a lawyer, he asked the Immigration authorities to leave. They did, but warned him he had only seven days in which to get a lawyer, and that they'd be back in a week.

Four days later, in the dead of night, Ricardo and three other detainees overwhelmed an unarmed guard in the men's dormitory of the El Paso Detention Center, took him hostage, and demanded his keys and intercom. The guard hesitated, but Ricardo had fashioned a makeshift knife from a metal bed frame. He ran it across the guard's neck, gave him a three-inch gash, and the guard complied. Moments later, Ricardo and his accomplices unlocked the Center's kitchen and, arming themselves with proper knives and a meat cleaver as well, made their hostage use the confiscated intercom to inform the guards outside that he was a prisoner. "Tell them to open the electrical gate," Ricardo ordered. "I'm wanted for murder, so don't fuck around, because I've got nothing to lose."

The hostage did as he was told, and his colleagues, fearing for his safety, opened the gate. Ricardo and his men came storming through it, locked up their hostage and the other guards, stole money and guns, and commandeering a car and a guard's uniform, succeeded in making their way across the border into Juarez. Soon afterward, Ricardo's accomplices were apprehended. But not

Ricardo. He had managed to board a train for Mexico City. "And that's where he met the next woman he's confessed to killing," Hines said. "Laura Gomez."

"Did she look like the other women he's said he killed?" I asked. "Long-haired, full-bodied?"

Hines shrugged. "We haven't been able to get a picture of her." Then he smiled and said triumphantly, "But I'll tell you what I do have. A picture of another woman who went out with Caputo. Kept a diary, too. And sent it to us."

He began rifling through his box of files and soon pulled out a large color photograph of Ricardo sitting at a restaurant table alongside a redheaded woman. "Ya know, our friend Ricardo struck me as very intelligent the night I spoke to him," he said as he waved the picture at me. "But he isn't so intelligent. Him or his lawyer, either. Because if they hadn't reached out for publicity and gotten all that press and TV, the LAPD wouldn't know about Devon Green. And we wouldn't know about *this* woman."

"Who is she?"

"Lotte Angstrom. Lives in Denmark now. But she used to live in L.A., and when the story about Caputo's return hit the papers, one of the friends she'd made in L.A. remembered that when she lived there, she'd gone out with an Argentinian guy. So the friend sent Angstrom some newspaper clippings about Caputo, and after she saw them, Angstrom sent me this picture—and her reminiscences."

Angstrom didn't look at all like the women Caputo had admitted murdering. Unlike them, her hair was short, her features coarse, and her clothing dowdy. But in one respect she reminded me of them. Mouth parted and eyes wide, she had a needy and trusting look about her. To me, it seemed the face of a woman eager to be liked and ready to believe only the best of others.

"Angstrom met Caputo when he was working at Scandia, one of L.A.'s top restaurants," Hines said. "She knew him as Bob Martin. Here—'October ninth, 1982. Met Bob, thirty-seven. Divorced. No children. From Argentina. Served in Vietnam. Lives with two men in a house.' "

"Lives with two men? Not his wife?" I said. "Inspector Sanders in San Francisco told me Ricardo was married when he worked at Scandia."

"Well, Ricardo didn't tell Angstrom anything about a wife. He just said he was living with two roommates. Who knows if it was true? Any more than that he had a lot of money, which he also told Angstrom."

"She believed that?"

"Yeah. And liked him. Dated him for a while. Spoke with him on the phone every day. Then she stopped hearing from him. She thought he'd gone back to Argentina, because that's what he'd said he was going to do. But then one night she went to Scandia again, and she saw him there. And realized he'd been conning her. 'He made great plans,' she wrote in her diary. 'And promises which he did not keep.' "

"Fascinating." I was reading between the lines, imagining Caputo telling Angstrom his family was wealthy, as he'd told Judith Becker's parents, and that he was going to inherit a ranch, as he'd told Barbara Taylor. I was imagining him promising Angstrom that if she helped him out with some money, he'd go home and claim his inheritance, then return for her and take her to the Andes to live a rich and exotic life.

Hines broke my reverie by saying, "Yeah, fascinating. But what's important are the dates. Dates are what you're always hoping to get in my business. And in this case, we got some, and they establish that in October of 1982 and in March and April of 1983, Caputo was working at Scandia."

"And going out with women," I exclaimed, remembering my conversation with Sanders about Jacqui. "Going out with women even when, according to him, he didn't do that kind of thing because he was married."

"Right."

"So maybe he went out with Jacqui that year, too."

"Possible."

Remembering that Gordon McEwan's informant had said that Caputo had been living up near 158th Street in New York around the time he killed Jacqui, I asked, "Could he have left Scandia and gone East to live? Could he have quit his job?"

"That's something we don't know. Angstrom sees Caputo for the last time on April eighth, 1983. After that, she doesn't see him anymore, or at least, she doesn't write about him anymore. So we have no way of knowing whether he was still at Scandia."

"What about his job records, time cards?"

"Scandia closed a few years ago," Hines sighed, "and the records can't be located. Was he at Scandia after April 1983? Was he still in L.A.? Was he living in the East? Was he living on the moon? Your guess is as good as mine."

Hines had been a fountain of information. After telling me about Angstrom, he'd filled me in about Devon Green, informing me that she'd wanted to become a model and had only gone to work at Scandia, where she'd become an apprentice chef, while waiting for her big break. "Her body was found, brutally beaten and partially clothed, in an empty lot off a highway," Hines had said. "The LAPD didn't know at the time they found her that she and Ricardo were friends. But they know it now. Because all that attention Ricardo got when he turned himself in made a witness come forward." Hines had chuckled at this, then said with elation, "Seems Devon used to hang out after work with a group of Scandia employees that went drinking and dancing in nearby clubs—and Ricardo was part of the group."

Hines had told me all this and shown me one of Green's modeling shots, a large color photograph showing a shapely woman with a jaunty nose, dove gray eyes, and a cascade of glossy amber-colored hair. But Hines hadn't known much about Caputo's last admitted victim, Laura Gomez, who'd been murdered in Mexico in 1977. When I'd asked about her again, he'd said, "I can't help you out there. Every time we talk to Mexico, the only thing they tell us is what they can't tell us. Partly it's the language barrier. Partly it's because the case is so old. But whatever it is, Mexico's giving us trouble."

9

Mexico was giving me trouble, too. I'd gotten the names of the relevant police inspectors down there, and I'd called and written and faxed them for information about Laura Gomez, but my calls and letters and faxes had gone unanswered. And then one day, as if miraculously, I received a thick packet of police reports. There was no sender's name, no one with whom to communicate. But the packet contained a vast amount of material about Ricardo's stay in Mexico and his eventual relationship with Gomez.

She wasn't his first girlfriend in Mexico. Leafing through the reports I'd been sent, I discovered that initially he'd bent his sights on a different woman, one Maria Lopez, a twenty-nine-year-old high-school-educated interior decorator who lived at home with her parents, religious Catholics. Ricardo had met her less than three months after escaping from El Paso and arriving in Mexico City and, after only a brief relationship, had asked her to marry him.

Maria didn't know much about Ricardo at the time. He'd told her that he was an American and that his name was Richard Cooper Roman. She'd doubted this. He hadn't seemed, she felt, like an American. But he'd shown her his driver's license, which did indeed identify him as Richard Roman, and he'd explained that he hadn't always been an American, that he'd begun his life as an Argentinian, only to be brought to the States by his parents when they and his sisters emigrated there. His parents? Maria had asked him. What were they like? His father was dead, Ricardo had replied. And as to his mother and even his sisters, he didn't have much to do with them anymore. Because they were prostitutes.

The young Mexican interior decorator was hesitant about marrying a man she'd known only a short while, and especially a man from a family like that. But at his suggestion, she took him home to meet *her* family. The visit reassured her. Ricardo, charming and garrulous as always, made the same kind of favorable impression on her parents that he'd made on the parents of so many of his victims, and after the visit Maria said yes, she would be his wife. Still, she wanted to wait until he had a good job. Ricardo dressed well and he had managed to purchase a sleek, expensive motorcycle. But he was apparently making his living merely by giving karate lessons. Maria wanted more in a husband.

Nevertheless, she agreed to a different proposal of his, agreed that while he was looking for work and they were waiting to wed, they take an apartment together. She needn't move in, he said to calm her fears about propriety. Not until they tied the knot. But he would live in the apartment and fix it up and get it ready for the time when she did become his bride.

Maria said yes and they went apartment hunting. Ricardo wanted a good address, and they found a place that pleased him, a terraced, three-room spread in Coyoacàn, a middle-class neighborhood not far from sites beloved by tourists, the

Universidad Nacional Autónoma de México, with
its Diego Rivera murals, and the Bosque de
Chapultepec, with its gardens, zoos, and museums.
But when they signed the lease, Ricardo insisted
they put it in Maria's name only. This worried her.
But since Ricardo said he would pay the rent, she
went along with his request and even agreed to
another—that she put the utilities in her name, too.

I learned all this from the reports of the Mexican
police, who had interviewed Maria shortly after the
murder of Laura Gomez, and I was struck by the
fact that in those reports, Maria came across as so
passive and acquiescent that she sounded positively
feather-brained. But I suppose that when she talked
to the police, she had some investment in presenting herself as foolishly good-natured and naive at
the time she started seeing Ricardo. It allowed her
to rationalize the fact that she had entered upon
what would soon prove a highly unpleasant relationship.

During it, Ricardo looked for work and Maria
came dutifully to the Coyoacàn apartment every day
to cook and clean for him. But Ricardo found no
work and soon became touchy and irritable. He
blew up at Maria, shouted at her, called her stupid.
More, he behaved mysteriously. One day he left
home for a few days and, when he returned, told her
that from now on, she should call him not Richard
Cooper Roman, but Ricardo Martinez Díaz.

To give Maria her due, she did manage to ask him
why. But when he responded, "Because I did some
bad things in the past and I want to forget them,"
she probed no further. So she never knew, she
claimed, what the Mexican police eventually found
out, which was that Ricardo and a friend of his had
traveled to a distant village, bribed an official there,
and obtained a false birth certificate and social

security card in the name of Ricardo Martinez Díaz. But perhaps Maria didn't want to know, wanted to look the other way. For at last, armed with proper identification, Ricardo got a job. He began working as a salesman for Time-Life Books.

Nevertheless, as the police reports I had received revealed, there was to be no wedding. Despite having a job, Ricardo's bad temper continued, and one day he punched Maria hard in the face. She wanted to leave him right then and there, but after he hit her, he sobbed and begged for her forgiveness. So she kept on coming to the apartment. But not long afterward they had another fight, this one about women. Other women. Ricardo told Maria that he didn't need her because he could have any woman he wanted and that in fact he'd been having some behind her back. Maria got hysterical and, unaware of how lucky she was to exit the relationship with just a few scratches and bruises, fled the apartment, leaving Ricardo in full possession of the few objects they'd purchased together.

I doubt that Ricardo regretted the departure of his fiancée. Indeed, I'm sure he welcomed that departure, for according to the reports I had received, he had by then met Laura Gomez, a woman he deemed far more desirable. Laura was younger than Maria, only twenty-three. She was better educated, a college graduate enrolled in a graduate program in industrial psychology at the nearby university. And her parents were rich. Her father, Fidel Gomez Martinez, owned one of Mexico's largest trucking companies.

Given this, Laura had been raised in the lap of luxury. The Gomezes lived in a neighborhood of Mexico City that resembled Beverly Hills, all sprawling mansions and lush gardens, and their house occupied almost an entire block. Out back, there was a large swimming pool, and in the garage, eleven cars, two of which, a Maverick and a sporty white Mustang, belonged to Laura herself. Laura's parents had wanted Laura and their only other child, an older girl named Miriam, to be sophisticated. They had taken them on trips to Europe, South America, and the United States. And they had sent Laura, who was artistic and loved to draw and paint, to college in California, at UCLA.

According to Ricardo, who after he turned himself in talked more admiringly of Laura than of his other murdered conquests, she was beautiful, the fairest of them all. A green-eyed woman with light brown hair that was almost blond, she had been chosen by an advertising agency to do television commercials for one of its clients, a beer called La Rubia Mejor, which means the best light beer but also the best blonde. Ricardo was to say that he met this telegenic beauty when he accompanied some friends to the TV studio where she was filming a commercial.

Why would so attractive and worldly a woman become involved with a Ricardo Caputo? Ricardo would explain it by saying that despite her beauty, wealth, and sophistication, Laura held herself in low esteem and feared that her parents preferred her sister. "In this, we were like twins," Ricardo would say.

But back to the police reports: they revealed that Laura was, like so many of Ricardo's victims, a nurturer, a giver. Soon after she met Ricardo, who was working at the time at his Time-Life job, he mentioned to her that he had higher ambitions than to be a mere book salesman, but that as a foreigner he was having trouble getting better work; Laura used her influence to win him a higher-paying position at a Mexican subsidiary of the Atlas steel company. And around that time, they became lovers.

Laura never told her parents that she and Ricardo had a sexual relationship. Nor did she ever introduce him to them. But they knew she was dating him and, or so they told the police, they weren't particularly worried about it. Their reason was that their home was full of housemaids who reported to them whenever this new friend of Laura's came to visit and said he and Laura always sat properly in the living room, looking at and talking about drawings he had penciled.

He was a friend from school, her parents told the police they had assumed. She had many of those, but no doubt she particularly liked this new young man because, like her, he was artistic.

But there was, of course, far more to Laura's relationship with Ricardo than a homebound mutual appreciation of art. Laura was seeing Ricardo outside the parental nest, was sleeping with him in the apartment he had once shared with Maria. And although Laura's parents would eventually say they were ignorant of the fact, Laura, like Natalie and Judith before her, became pregnant.

On a Friday afternoon in September 1977, she mentioned casually to her parents that her friend Ricardo had invited her to attend a karate exhibition in the evening and asked their permission to join him. They themselves were going out to a conference and dinner that night, and they agreeably said yes.

Laura spent the afternoon at home, then toward evening got dressed. She put on a skirt, a white blouse with a mandarin collar, and a gold ring studded with three diamonds. Ricardo arrived for her in a taxi around 8 P.M. Her parents had already left, but the housekeeper answered the doorbell. Laura, bidding the housekeeper good-bye, told her she and Ricardo were going directly to the exhibition and got into the taxi.

That was the last time she was seen alive. She and Ricardo didn't go to a karate exhibition but went instead to his apartment, and there he killed her.

I read the details with dismay. Ricardo ripped off Laura's clothes, dragged her from room to room throughout the apartment, burned her body in several places with cigarettes, and beat her about the head and face with his fists. Then he picked up a steel bar and smashed it down on her skull no fewer than ten times, bashing in her forehead and jaw so that her teeth went rocketing from their cradle of bone. The disbursement of her teeth had prompted the Mexican press to report initially that before Ricardo killed Gomez, he had tortured her, pulled her teeth. Gordon McEwan had read those first accounts, which was why he'd told me about the teeth. But the Mexican police report suggested that Ricardo hadn't pulled them out, just knocked them out.

It makes little difference. Just as I had imagined when McEwan told me about Laura's death, those teeth, little pearls encrusted with blood, lay scattered across the floor.

Reading, I wished the reports said less about Laura's destruction and more about her relationship with Ricardo. Had she, like Natalie, Judith, and Barbara, become disillusioned with her handsome lover? Had she, like them, been planning to break up with him? Had she hidden from him the fact that she was pregnant, as Judith had done? Had she told him she was pregnant, as Natalie had done and later denied? Or had she perhaps told him she was pregnant but said that the father was someone else, thereby arousing Ricardo's jealous fury?

There was no information that could help me answer those questions. But something indicated a surprising similarity between Ricardo's movements on the day he killed Laura Gomez and his movements on the day he killed Judith Becker. The similarity was that, just as he had closed down his bank account before murdering Judith, he had taken out some loans immediately before murdering Laura.

To me, that information suggested that Ricardo was getting ready to leave town, just as he had before murdering Judith, and that on the eve of his departure he had asked Laura, just as he appears to have asked Judith, for something she hadn't wanted to grant him, a refusal that triggered his rage. As with Judith, I surmised, it could have been something material. But what? One of her cars? Her diamond ring? And then, buried in the Mexican police reports, I saw a little statement about that ring. It was missing when they found her body. The only thing on or in her hands were ripped-out clumps of Ricardo's hair

He had made no effort to disentangle them from her fingers. Nor had he attempted to retrieve his possessions from the apartment. He had simply cleared out and, once again, totally and effectively vanished.

After learning about Gomez and putting together my new knowledge with what I'd already learned about Brown, Becker, and Taylor, it was impossible for me to entertain even for a moment the notion that Ricardo was a schizophrenic. Schizophrenics are disorganized, have confused and chaotic thoughts. Ricardo's thinking had been shrewd and organized. In his relationships with each of the women he had admitted killing, he had been manipulative, asking them for money or other assistance. And after each killing except for that of Natalie Brown, he had covered his tracks, disappeared in a most skillful fashion.

An insanity defense? I said to myself when I put down the packet of papers. Ridiculous.

10

But an insanity defense was still what Kennedy was apparently planning. In December 1994 there was another hearing to determine if Ricardo's statements to the police on the night he killed Natalie could be considered to have been fairly gotten, and this time it was the defense's turn to call witnesses. Kennedy put on a mental health expert—not Dr. Park Dietz, the famed psychiatrist who had videotaped his examination of Ricardo, but a man named Sanford Drob, a psychologist who had given Ricardo psychological tests and studied his Matteawan and Manhattan State Hospital records. Dr. Drob's view was that Ricardo's statements should be disallowed, for, "three weeks after his arrest," he asserted, "he was diagnosed with a serious psychotic disorder."

Elise McCarthy, sitting at the prosecution table, began scribbling energetically. She had asked to have this hearing delayed because the defense had only three days ago supplied her with the notes on which Dr. Drob would be basing his testimony. But the judge, John Dunne, had ruled against her, saying he'd give her a few weeks to prepare her cross-examination of the psychologist but that his direct testimony had to be heard today.

Drob was expansive, prolix. "When you talk with Mr. Caputo," he said, "he presents, particularly at this point, as an intelligent, verbal individual. But his scores on a wide variety of tests of perceptual functioning, intellectual functioning, abstract ability—let's forget construction ability where he does better than the fiftieth percentile—but in perceptual functioning and abstract reasoning and general intellectual functioning, his scores all cluster between the tenth and twenty-fifth percentile, which doesn't make him mentally deficient but significantly below average on these measures. For example, his IQ is measured at a full scale of eighty, which is just at the cusp between the low normal and borderline level of intellectual functioning."

Kennedy knew that the court-appointed psychiatrist who had found Ricardo competent to stand trial had described him as a faker or malingerer. And he knew, too, that however long-windedly Drob was expressing himself, he was reporting a discrepancy between Ricardo's highly intelligent manner and his dismally low scores on intelligence tests. It was a potentially harmful discrepancy, one that could support the notion of Ricardo's being a faker by suggesting he had made an effort to do poorly on Drob's tests, that he had purposefully feigned dim-wittedness. So Kennedy attempted damage control and asked Drob directly if he thought Caputo was a malingerer.

"No," Drob answered with merciful brevity.

"Why not?" Kennedy asked.

"Well, there are three reasons," Drob said. "The first is that he was in hospitals for over three years and found incompetent for over three years. The second is that my own psychological testing shows that without question this is a seriously disturbed psychotic schizophrenic individual. And the third reason I have is a kind of commonsense reason. Mr. Caputo was living in Mexico, apparently without any reason to turn himself in. Yet he voluntarily and on his own did so, as a result of haunting nightmares and perceptual and hallucinatory experiences that gave him to believe that the only way that he himself could gain peace with his own mind would be to turn himself in for these previous crimes, which had now come back to him and were given to haunting him.

"For an individual to do that, to come clean, if you will, with all of these crimes and all of this horror that has been his life, and now fake a mental illness, would be very unusual, if just inconceivable in my mind."

"Come clean!" Elise McCarthy was beside herself when I spoke to her after the hearing. "Caputo hasn't come clean. Hines has turned up all sorts of dirt about him. Him and that sweet little wife of his. The one who went on *PrimeTime* and said he was the nicest, kindest man in the world."

"What kind of dirt?"

"False documents. Unpaid bills. Fleeing the country with illegal funds. I'm talking about recent stuff—things that happened long after the time Caputo claims to have stopped killing and begun living a so-called respectable life."

With McCarthy's help, as well as with that of Hines, I was able to piece together the outlines of that life, to learn that after leaving his first wife, the one who had vanished, Ricardo had in the mid-1980s fetched up in Guadalajara, Mexico. There he had again gotten new identity papers, and with them landed a job as an English instructor in a privately owned language school. And there he had begun dating the woman who would become his second wife and speak up for him on *PrimeTime*, a seventeen-year-old beauty queen named Susana Elizondo, whose coronation had netted her many prizes, among them a six-month course of English lessons at Ricardo's school.

He was twenty years Susana's senior, but as was his wont, he proposed marriage—even though he had never divorced his first wife. Susana didn't know this. Nor did she know much about Ricardo at all. In fact, she thought his name was Roberto Dominguez, which was the name on his identity cards. But like Felicia Fernandez, she, too, married him and, in her case, remained with him until he turned himself in.

They lived first in Mexico, then in Chicago, where Ricardo got a job at Harry Caray's, a famous restaurant in downtown Chicago. "It was owned by an announcer for the Chicago Cubs," McCarthy told me one day in her office, a cell-like space as dreary as the conference room in which we'd met earlier. "The kind of place that's popular with sports figures." Then, "Law enforcement types, too," she added ironically.

"You mean that while the FBI and Interpol were searching for Ricardo all over the world, he was living right here among us? Working in a place where the police ate lunch?"

"Yes. And if you think that's something, wait'll you hear about Caputo's house. Somehow or other he got his hands on enough money to buy a little house in Cicero, on the outskirts of Chicago. And guess what? The house was right across the street from a police station."

We were both surprised by how casual Ricardo had become, how sure he was that he wouldn't be caught. And as McCarthy continued to fill me in about this period of Ricardo's life, I found myself even more surprised by how normal, how ordinary, that life seemed. I'd always been fascinated by people who'd led double lives and had frequently written about them, but none of the grand impostors whose lives I'd explored in the past were as skillful at concealing their secret sides as Ricardo, who had become a master at deception.

His house in Cicero had only a tiny scrap of yard and narrow strip of alleyway separating it from its neighbors. Ricardo made friends among the families who lived in the nearby houses and conducted himself, when he was around them, like any suburban family man. He went to their backyard barbecues, held a few of his own, borrowed and lent groceries, and paid the local teenagers to baby-sit for his and Susana's three children. He also helped his neighbors with home repairs, lending them tools and offering to hang kitchen cabinets, nail together bookcases. Not that he was a model of propriety—he drank, heavily at times, and sometimes he frequented nudie bars. But so did other suburban family men.

At work, too, according to McCarthy, he made friends, seemed like a regular enough sort of fellow. He even won the admiration of his bosses. "Harry Caray's conducted periodic evaluations of its staff," McCarthy informed me. "And you should see his early marks!"

"His marks?"

"Yes." She pulled a photocopied form from a folder on her desk and handed it to me. The form, designed for the evaluation of Harry Caray staff members, had boxes in which a supervisor could rate an employee's skills and abilities, and it had been filled out shortly after Ricardo, who was using the name Franco Porraz, had started working at the restaurant. For Attitude, a supervisor had given Ricardo a 5 out of 5, the highest grade. For Job

Knowledge, he had given him another 5 out of 5. For Quantity of Service, again a 5. For Dependability, a 4. The supervisor was pleased with Ricardo's performance, and in an area at the bottom of the form where comments could be made, he had written that the new waiter was a "true professional."

Sometime later, I obtained through Detective Hines the name and phone number of Ricardo's supervisor. He was Steve Borchew, a general manager of Harry Caray's. Borchew hadn't hired Ricardo, but he'd been present when another manager did so, and he'd given his approval to the selection.

"I looked over Franco's résumé—we knew him as Franco—and it was very impressive," Borchew told me. "He listed all these fine restaurants he'd worked in—there were some in New York, as I recall, and some in Hawaii and L.A. And I talked to Franco. Liked him. So I said, yeah, let's take him on. I trusted my judgment about people back then. Still do. No, still try to. I mean, I've been general manager here for seven years. And now I'm telling myself that no matter what, even when you check the references, it doesn't mean anything. You just can't know. But you can't live with yourself if you're thinking that all the time. You gotta have trust."

I said, "Yes. If you can."

"Yeah, well . . . but hey, crazy people make some of the best waiters."

According to Borchew, Ricardo had definitely been one of Harry Caray's best, at least at first. He'd been fast, efficient, and so ingratiating that customers used to ask to be seated at his station. He'd also shown a talent for winning the periodic competitions the restaurant sponsored among its waiters—competitions to see who could sell the most of a particular dessert or a particular dinner special. And he'd been exceedingly considerate toward certain members of the restaurant's staff—the female staff members. When one of them had said she wanted to repaint her kitchen, he'd volunteered to help; when another had needed assistance in moving from one apartment to another, he'd offered to provide it; and frequently, when women waiters had complained about their aching backs and shoulders, he'd given them back rubs. "One of the women waiters told me," Borchew said, " 'Franco's got the best hands. Absolutely the best!' "

Borchew paused to let me marvel at the irony of this, then went on, "So, like I said, I didn't see anything wrong with him. Not for a long time. But then we started getting complaints. A customer said Franco had given him the wrong change when he paid his bill. Another one said he hadn't made clear that there was going to be an extra charge for dessert. Someone else said he brought and opened up for them some additional bottles of wine when they hadn't been ordered. He was doing what we call gouging the customers—driving up the price of the check so his tip would be proportionately higher.

"So I spoke to him about these things, put them in his evaluations, and warned him to stop. But he didn't stop, he kept it up. And the complaints kept coming. And finally, when he'd been here about three and a half years, we told him that we were putting him on probation and that if we got one more complaint, he'd be terminated. Then we got one, and I had to fire him."

"What was that like?"

"Scary. He didn't explode or anything, but he got this look in his eyes. I'd seen something like it before. Once, he'd had a run-in with another waiter and he'd gotten a real mean look in his eyes and

said, 'Keep this guy out of my way, or I'll kill him.'
And I'd kept them apart, because, hey, waiters are
excitable. But the way he looked then was like nothing compared to how he looked the day I fired him.
I mean, I was glad to see the back of him, because
you could see he was real bothered."

After he was fired from Harry Caray's, Ricardo
decided to move again. Detective Hines told me that
part of the story: "Ricardo had bought himself a
slew of household goods on credit. Television sets.
Kitchen appliances. He wasn't making payments,
and American Express was dunning him. For more
than ten thousand dollars. So maybe that's why he
made up his mind to go—we don't know for sure,
but what we do know is that about a month after he
was fired, he sold his house, put fifty thousand dollars in his bank account, and bought Susana and
the kids plane tickets to Mexico City."

What happened next almost resulted in Ricardo's
capture. Susana went to O'Hare Airport, but before
she could board her plane, she was stopped by U.S.
customs officials conducting a routine currency
check. They asked for identification and Susana
showed them a social security card. They also asked
how much money she was transporting, and she
told them she had two thousand dollars. But for
some reason, the customs officials were suspicious
of her and insisted on searching her purse. When
they did, they discovered she was concealing an
additional thirteen thousand. And they also discovered that the social security number she had given
them was registered to someone else. "A dead white
baby boy!" Hines exclaimed, leveling his steely gaze
on me. "That innocent little wife of Ricardo's, that
mouthpiece for him on *PrimeTime Live*, was going
around with fake identification. Just like him."

"Maybe that's what kept her safe," I interrupted Hines. "I mean, she's the only woman we know about who got close to Ricardo and didn't get murdered. Or attacked. Or have to disappear. Maybe she had to go along with him to ensure her survival."

Hines had little sympathy for that view. "Yeah, well, she survived all right," he brushed it off. "But she didn't have to go on national television and paint Caputo like a saint. 'The man I married would never have harmed anyone,' or whatever that garbage she said was." Then, "Anyway, she didn't just use false ID," he went on harshly. "Or try to leave the country with hidden funds. She also lied to Customs, told them the money they'd found on her was legitimately hers, part of the proceeds from the sale of her and her husband's house."

"And it wasn't?"

"Well, she didn't try very hard to get it back. Customs confiscated the money and told her if she wanted it returned, she should file an affidavit. So she gets on her plane and later she tells Ricardo, who's still in the U.S., to file the affidavit. But he doesn't go through with it. I mean, he starts, he sends Customs this notarized affidavit on behalf of Franco Porraz and his wife. But right after he turns it in, he has second thoughts, realizes he's asking for trouble. And by the time Customs attempts to verify the facts, she's nowhere to be found. Neither is he."

Where was he? Mexico, again, it developed. "He joined Susana there," Hines said, "had another baby with her, and got a job as a salesman—a job that had him going back and forth between the United States and Mexico."

"What was he selling?"

"Medical supplies. He claims."

"Sounds like drugs to me."

Hines didn't comment, just continued, speaking

Who Killed Jacqui Bernard?

The man in this photo, Ricardo (Ricky or Richie) Caputo, is a strong suspect in the murder of Jacqueline Bernard on August 2, 1983. He has also used aliases Robert Diaz or Robert Ruiz, as well as other names.

Caputo is also wanted in connection with the murders of two other women. He was born in Argentina and is 32 years old. He is 5'7" or 5'8", 150–160 pounds, and has brown hair and eyes. These photos were taken about 10 years ago, and he may have grown a mustache. His hair may be thinning.

Caputo has worked as a waiter and busboy on the West Side of New York City. He is intelligent and well-spoken. He speaks several languages and is artistic. He may have met Jacqueline Bernard a few months before her death at an outing, party, or trip, or at a bar on the West Side. She may have been helping him with legal problems. He may have borrowed her car on the night of her murder or on other occasions.

If you have any information about Caputo, if you can identify the occasion on which he met Jacqueline Bernard, if you saw them together, or if you can recall any conversation regarding him, please call Gordon McEwan at   Jonathan Gordon Investigations. All information will be kept strictly confidential.

Please circulate this letter among the friends of Jacqueline Bernard and the organizations with which she was connected.

This poster, showing Ricardo as a young man, was circulated throughout New York City in 1985, two years after the murder of Jacqui Bernard.

Natalie Brown

Judith Becker

Barbara Taylor

Laura Gomez

Jacqui Bernard

Ricardo Caputo at his first communion,
at about age nine

Ricardo as a
teenager in
Argentina

Ricardo shortly
after arriving
in New York in
the late 1960s

Ricardo in
Barbara Taylor's
San Francisco
apartment

Some of the
many faces of
Ricardo Caputo

Ricardo in 1994, shortly after he turned himself in

with the bitterness that law enforcement people often manifest when talking about the ineffectualness of some of their peers, "So there he is in Mexico, going back and forth. Back and forth. And no one figures out who he is. Not till he shows up in Argentina and all on his lonesome breaks the news to the world himself."

I was in the process of gathering these details when, in the middle of January 1995, I received an unexpected call from Elise McCarthy. "They want a plea!" she told me excitedly. "They've been calling all morning and saying they want a plea."

"Won't that make it hard for Kennedy to argue insanity in Caputo's other cases?" I asked, remembering that she'd once told me this consideration would stand in the way of the lawyer's going for a plea in her case.

"Kennedy's pulling out," she said. "A legal aid attorney is going to handle Caputo in Westchester."

"Legal aid!" I exclaimed. "What happened? Why's Kennedy quitting?"

"I guess Dietz has refused to find Caputo insane," McCarthy trilled, sounding positively jubilant.

I felt pleased by the news, too. If Kennedy is pulling out, I thought, maybe he'll finally be willing to speak with me. And if he does, maybe I'll be able to press him about helping me get in touch with Ricardo's brother, Alberto. I was keen to do so. I'd learned so much about Ricardo, and yet I felt I didn't know him. I needed to speak to people who did. To his mother. His father. His brother. After months of calling around, I'd turned up no one I knew, other than Kennedy, who knew Alberto. And one day, I'd finally done what I hate to do—called him up out of the blue. I hadn't gotten ten past his secretary. After making me state my name and business, she'd said that Mr. Caputo wasn't taking calls from members of the press. Kennedy could get me a better reception.

"Caputo allegedly tried to commit suicide last week," McCarthy was going on. "Saved up a bunch of pills and swallowed them."

I tried to keep my mind on the matter at hand. "How is he?" I inquired.

"Okay. I doubt it was a serious effort. He probably just wanted attention." Her prosecutorial scorn must have reminded her to be a little less open with me, for then she returned to the subject of the plea, saying, "Of course, you realize there's no deal yet. We're just thinking it over."

"Sure." Still, I figured the plea had already been worked out. District attorneys, no matter how open they seem to be, never tell you something that's going to happen, only that which has already happened.

Two weeks later on an unseasonably warm and springlike day at the tail end of January, Judge Dunne explained to a sparse handful of spectators and press people that Caputo would be pleading guilty to manslaughter in the first degree and receiving the maximum sentence for that crime. Then Dunne questioned the once-handsome defendant, who was even more paunchy and glabrous than usual.

"How old are you?" Dunne asked.

"Forty-five." He looked so much older that I found it hard to believe.

"Are you under the influence of any drugs?"

"No."

"Are you suffering from any mental disability that would affect your ability to take a plea?"

"No."

A moment later, Judge Dunne asked Caputo to state in his own words what he had done.

"I stabbed Natalie to death," he whispered, his words so muffled that they seemed to be coming from underwater. "And I was very emotionally disturbed at the time."

"Did you intend to cause her death?" Elise McCarthy, rising, asked coldly.

"Yes."

And that was that, the brisk, anticlimactic resolution of a murder that had preoccupied Ed Brown, Judy Epstein, James Gay, and a host of Natalie's friends and relatives for twenty-four years. None of them were present. They had not been alerted to attend, for a plea, no matter how carefully worked out and assiduously agreed upon, is never a sure thing until the defendant actually announces in open court that he'll take it. Nor was Alberto Caputo present. Ricardo had only Kennedy on his side.

The tall, well-tailored attorney offered Ricardo some lawyerly comfort, patting him on the back of the gray sweatshirt that had replaced the sleek leather jacket he used to wear to court. And then Ricardo was led away, while Kennedy went into the corridor to face the usual barrage of questions.

"Why did you give up the insanity defense?" a television reporter asked him.

"I can't comment on that," he said.

"Did you advise Caputo to plead guilty to manslaughter or was it his own decision?" another reporter asked.

"I can't comment on that."

"Is there anything you *can* comment about?" asked a third.

"Only this. That whether he goes to a jail or a hospital, he'll be treated by a psychiatrist and psychotherapist, and he'll remain on medication wherever he goes."

What medication was that? No one asked, and I didn't either, just added the question to the burgeoning list of unknowns about Caputo—the blank in the center of my canvas—that I carried in my head. But I was more determined than ever to try to fill in that blank, and as soon as Kennedy ended his press conference, I went over to him and once again asked if we could make an appointment.

"No problem," he said. "Just call me in the office and we'll set it up."

Well, that's progress, I thought. But just as before, when I called, he didn't call back.

I called a second time. And a third. Still no call back.

"What'll I do?" I moaned one day to a friend, a gossip columnist whose business it was to get the hard-to-reach to talk to her.

"Just phone him every morning," she said. "You know, you brush your teeth, have your coffee, call this guy."

I did that for about four weeks. I also wrote to him. Still, he didn't get back to me. And then finally, I received a note from Kennedy's secretary: "Mr. Kennedy wanted to let you know," she wrote, "that he will talk to you at the sentencing."

11

The day of Ricardo's sentencing dawned windy and cool, but it was brilliantly sunny, true spring at last, and later that morning as I trekked the few blocks between the Mineola station and Nassau's courthouse, I thought I detected a decidedly festive air in the streets. Certainly, there was such an air outside Judge Dunne's courtroom, for the media, partying on containers of coffee, sticky buns, and muffins, had returned in some semblance of force.

Perhaps the editors and news show producers were there because, like the Hungarian psychiatrist who first identified the phenomenon and for whom it was named, they subscribed to the theory that most people crave the Zeigarnik effect, the experience of closure. But more likely it was simply because sentencings make good copy, good footage, offering as they do at least a minor sop to the appetites of a public once addicted to hangings and still hungry for the spectacle of punishment being meted out.

In any case, the crowds were so thick that I had to elbow my way into the courtroom, where, as soon as I saw Kennedy, I made a beeline for him and said, "Your secretary tells me that you're finally going to talk to me today."

Kennedy must have forgotten. Or maybe he'd never intended to see me. "I'm sorry but I can't," he said. "I've got to be in a Manhattan court right after this sentencing."

"Let me come with you," I pressed him anyway. "We can talk en route."

"No," he shook his head. "I just don't have the time today."

"What about tomorrow, then?" I was embarrassed by my brazen, if futile, pursuit of Kennedy, but I had no intention of abandoning it. For one thing, I could see no good reason for him to deny me a few minutes of his time, however precious it was. For another, I was beginning to enjoy the game he and I had been playing all year—his resistance, my relentlessness. It was almost comical, an amusing contest he and I had devised to lighten the drudgeries of our respective occupations.

He won this round, won it as he'd won all the others, by appearing to give me the win. "All right, all right," he said. "Call me in my office at four o'clock, and if I'm there, you can come over."

I nodded as if I actually believed he'd be there, and took a seat. The courtroom was filling up, mostly with reporters and camerapeople, but here and there with people I'd interviewed, people whose lives had been devastated by Ricardo. I noticed a good friend of Jacqui Bernard's, an older woman who was sitting in a back pew, looking frail and tense. I saw Judith Becker's sister, Janie, sitting up front with eyes that looked red from crying. And I spotted Ed Brown, his generally mobile face set in an unsmiling, stony mask. For the first time in twenty and twenty-four years, respectively, Janie and Ed would once again be seeing Ricardo, this man whom they had once liked and considered an appropriate suitor for their sisters. Janie was there out of curiosity, I supposed. Not Ed. He was going to be called upon to address the court.

He did so almost as soon as an equally unsmiling Ricardo was led in and the proceedings got under way. "I know you have limitations on what you can and can't recommend in terms of sentencing," Ed told Judge Dunne, "but I want you to do whatever you can to make sure that Caputo is never again free. My parents are dead, sir. But while they were alive, they lived in a prison that this man created— a prison of grief." At this, Ed paused and cast a baleful glance at Ricardo, who offered him no sign of recognition. Then he turned back to the judge and said, "It was a prison from which they never even had a chance to apply for parole."

Kennedy spoke next, rising magisterially and quickly commanding the attention of the room with his powerful voice. "Your Honor, Mr. Caputo is a man who was brutalized as a child. Raped as a child. Abandoned as a child. I am not saying that these things excuse his conduct. I am saying them in the hopes that the court, and maybe the public, and maybe even, with God's help, Mr. Brown will be able to see Mr. Caputo's crimes in a context."

Kennedy's connection to Ricardo was rapidly drawing to an end. But he still felt an obligation to speak up for him, and to do it with as little acknowledgment of the damning information about Ricardo that the prosecution and police had turned up as he could. "Mr. Caputo and Natalie Brown were to be married," he said, although that declaration, based on an assertion of Ricardo's, had been disputed to the prosecution by Ed Brown and Natalie's friends. "And for reasons that none of us can fully comprehend, he killed her," the lawyer went on. "And he killed again. And again. Then, seventeen years passed, Judge, seventeen years during which he

maintained—and here is the most extraordinary
aspect of this gentleman's complex personality or
personalities—he maintained a good job and a family relationship." Again, it was a statement that
seemed based more on Ricardo's version of his life
than on what Detective Hines had determined.

After that, Kennedy waxed eloquent. "And then
fifteen months ago, he began having recurrent
nightmares, recurrent flashbacks, recurrent memories of these terrible, terrible homicides. And at a
time in his life when he could theoretically have
stayed free, he chose to voluntarily come in. Why?
Because as he said publicly . . .'I would rather that
my body be in jail and my mind free than have my
mind in jail, as it is now, with a free body.' Now,
that's an extraordinary thing. That's a great service
to society. And I respectfully suggest that it deserves
Your Honor's consideration. And there's a second
thing about him that I think is significant for Your
Honor's consideration. It's his obvious remorse.
When he came to my office, he said, 'I want to make
a public statement because I believe that after I turn
myself in, I will never get an opportunity to publicly
apologize to the families of the victims for all their
pain.' And he did that."

Behind Kennedy, Janie Becker was weeping at
those inadequate words. But the lawyer didn't turn,
just continued urging the judge to be compassion-
ate, concluding his remarks with, "I won't presume
to tell you what sentence to give here. You have
passed on these kinds of things many times. But
this is a unique circumstance."

A moment later, Kennedy requested the court's
permission to allow his client to speak and, obtaining it, stood alongside Ricardo as he murmured a
brief apology. "Well, I turned myself in, Your Honor,
in order to avoid any more killings. And I wanted to

say to the families of the victims that I am very sorry because of what I did. I was sick, and I hope that now that I am to be incarcerated, I can be cured. That's all I've got to say."

The usually gentle-looking Judge Dunne had a cold look in his eyes. "All right," he announced, "there being no one else, it finally comes down to myself to make a determination in this particular case." The courtroom, already quiet, grew even stiller, and Dunne launched into his sentencing speech. His tone was hesitant at first. "This was not an easy decision to make because there appear to be many complications here that are unusual even in criminal court. I was, for example, troubled by the question of remorse. Was there true remorse here or was this just simply more of the manipulation that has been referred to in the various probation reports and psychiatric notes and conclusions?"

At this, Dunne's voice gained strength, and casting his cold eyes on Ricardo, he began speaking with a passion that bordered on fervor. "But I have reached a conclusion—which is that you, Mr. Caputo, are a brutal and cunning man. Your hollow statement to the national press, 'I want to come in and face my past,' shows not remorse but manipulation. Your claim that you would rather have your body locked up and your mind free can only be viewed as a transparent and plastic attempt to curry public and professional sympathy. And your wish, stated to the Nassau County Probation Department, that you want only to serve your obligation to this court and then return home to Argentina is what you are all about. Having led a life of murder, mayhem, and manipulation for these past twenty-five years, it's obviously your belief that a few words of sympathy and mea culpa will make you free. But to the extent that this court can, your home, to the hour of your last breath, shall be of stone and steel. This step today should only be the first of two, three, or four jail sentences, which consecutively and together, shall lead to the end of your life and beyond. Your past you have devoted to murderish self-gratification, causing permanent pain and irreplaceable loss to others. Now, may your haunting recollections cause you the same pain and punishment during a lifetime of incarceration."

Dunne then sentenced Ricardo to the maximum sentence he was able, under the law, to impose— eight and a third to twenty-five years in prison.

That afternoon, at four precisely, I called Kennedy, not expecting him to be in, just as part of our game. To my astonishment, his secretary said, "Mr. Kennedy left word that if you can get over here right away, he'll give you forty-five minutes." Was it another false promise? I couldn't risk thinking it was and, speeding out of my apartment, hailed a cab for Park Avenue, where Kennedy had his office.

When I arrived there, I still fully expected to be told he'd been called away, but a receptionist said, "Go right in. He's waiting for you."

That was an exaggeration. He was on the phone. But he was there. And so was I. At long last.

Waiting for him to get off the phone, I began to question whether talking with him would actually net me what I wanted—access to people who knew Ricardo. Probably not, I told myself; I was probably just wasting my time.

Still, it was interesting to be in Kennedy's baronial office, a huge room with huge windows that looked west across Park Avenue and south to lower Manhattan, offering the most extensive views of Manhattan's skyline that I had ever seen from one office. More, the place was exquisitely furnished.

The carpeted floors were overlaid with Oriental rugs, there were couches made from antique brass beds, and desks and tables and bookcases of glowing, burnished wood.

I wasn't at all surprised by the opulence. A lawyer's pursuit of personal happiness, Kennedy had once advised the actor Raúl Julia when he was preparing to act the part of a lawyer in the film *Presumed Innocent*, involved "winning or at least getting paid a lot while losing."

I had plenty of time to remember that remark, as well as others of his I'd read, for Kennedy was still on the phone. I sat down at an inlaid table and waited for him to finish.

When he did, he was extraordinarily entertaining, filled with anecdotes about a European trip he'd recently made. I'd known he was famous for having that top-of-the-trade lawyer's ability to amuse, enchant, and had even seen a bit of it during our previous brief encounters. Now I feared that in view of the battle of wills that had ended in my being, finally, in his office, he'd prove himself the ultimate victor by consuming with small talk the time he had promised to allot me. So I plunged into questioning him: "Are you disappointed in how the case turned out?" I asked. It wasn't what I really wanted to know, which was whether he'd put me in touch with Ricardo's family. But I didn't want to ask that first.

"I don't regret having taken the case, if that's what you mean," Kennedy said. "I've always been interested in the insanity defense and in diminished capacity."

"Why didn't you take the case to trial?"

"I realized that I didn't have the evidence to prove that back in 1971 Caputo was not responsible. And Park Dietz couldn't say with any certainty whether

Caputo was legally insane back in 1971. Of course, he couldn't say with certainty that he was sane, either. He just couldn't be definite one way or the other."

"Is Caputo disappointed?"

"He's pleased with what he got. Kvetch that he is. Of course, he'd rather have gone to trial."

A while later, I asked Kennedy to tell me about the *PrimeTime Live* show.

"I received more praise and more criticism for that than for anything else I've ever done in my life," he said. "And there are plenty of things for which I've received lots of praise or lots of criticism. But this was different. Because this had never been done before. It was the first time, but I guarantee you it won't be the last. Because it was a tactic all of us lawyers have to think about in this age of media, when everyone is basing everything they know on what they've seen on television. More and more, we lawyers have to think of preemptive ways to influence what happens with our clients. And this is a good way. It de-demonizes the client."

That Ricardo *was* demonic hardly mattered in this prescription. What mattered to Kennedy, I felt, was what always matters to defense attorneys, presenting their clients, no matter how execrable, in the best light possible, an ethic of the legal profession that strikes a great many of us, no matter how accustomed to it we become, as immoral. A part of me wanted to raise this with Kennedy, wanted to debate the value of a trade that demands such cunning of its practitioners. But, I'd best not provoke Kennedy, I cautioned myself. Not if I want his help in gaining access to Ricardo's family. And, exercising the cunning that my own profession often requires, I repressed the urge to be contentious and asked Kennedy a few questions about Caputo's surrender.

"The police hate the person who turns himself in," he said in answer to one of them. "Because they don't get the collar. They don't get the credit. We call the detectives who are out there searching for people who've disappeared the dogs, or we say they're on dog duty. Because they're sniffing, trying to get a trail. The people on dog duty hate it when someone voluntarily turns himself in."

Voluntarily? I thought. But what about that article in *Clarín*, the one that said Caputo had told someone he was being hunted in Mexico—if that was true, his surrender was hardly voluntary.

Kennedy was still talking. "The people on dog duty particularly hate it when it turns out the people they're hunting for are living in circumstances where the police *should* have gotten them, living right among us." And he was still dwelling on the elective nature of Caputo's surrender. "You hear all this garbage. Like that Caputo turned himself in because he was on *America's Most Wanted* and he was afraid someone might have seen the show and identified him and that he'd be caught. I mean, come on, how many people in Mexico, which was where he was when that show was aired, watch *America's Most Wanted?*"

I'm hearing an argument about Caputo's willingness to come in and take his punishment that Kennedy would have made in court, it occurred to me. I'm hearing the summation he'd have delivered if Caputo had been tried. But I'm like an obdurate juror. I don't believe it. Any more than I believe that putting Caputo on *PrimeTime Live*—"de-demonizing the client," Kennedy had called it—served some kind of high, idealistic purpose.

But there's no percentage in bringing up my dubiousness, I said to myself. Besides, it's growing late. And suspecting we might have exceeded my allotted forty-five minutes, "Caputo's brother," I leaped at last. Kennedy had already told me about how Alberto Caputo, a friend of a friend of his, had called him and sought his help in the matter of Ricardo. "The brother," I raced. "I want to ask you about the brother."

"What about him?" Kennedy sounded impatient and I glanced down at my watch. We *had* talked for more than three-quarters of an hour.

"Whether you'll call him for me." I laid my cards on the table. "Tell him I'm doing a book and want to speak to him."

Kennedy snorted. "Me call the brother? He doesn't speak to me anymore."

I groaned. Kennedy smiled. And then, as if he'd been jousting with me again, he said, "The brother still talks to my assistant, however. And while there's no guarantee he'll talk to *you*, I'll ask her to call him for you."

I was out of there seconds later, trying to hail a cab in Park Avenue's hectic rush-hour traffic and thinking gloomily of all the times Kennedy had promised to call me and failed to do so, all the times he'd said he'd see me but failed to do so. But he did finally see me, I buoyed myself as a taxi disgorged a passenger right in front of my feet. Maybe I'm getting lucky.

Three days later, as I was dozing over a book, I picked up my clamoring phone to hear a silken voice with a trace of a sibilant Latin American accent say, "I'm Alberto Caputo. I hear you want to speak to me."

I was immediately alert. "Mr. Caputo!" I exclaimed. "How good of you to call me."

"You're writing a book?"

"Yes," I murmured.

"About my brother?"

"Yes."

"And why should I speak to you?"

It was a question for which I had no ready answer. I've never known why people should speak to me, or to any writer for that matter. But they do. Time after time, even when it seems to serve no purpose except gratifying a need for attention, they do. "I don't know why," I admitted to Mr. Caputo. "And I must tell you that my book won't be sympathetic to your brother. I think he killed a friend of mine. But I am trying to understand him."

"Me, too," Alberto Caputo said. "I have been trying all my life." Then: "Perhaps"—he laughed, a deep purr of a laugh—"I will help you and you will help me."

PART TWO
RICARDO

12

Alberto Caputo and I had numerous telephone conversations before we actually set an interview date. From the beginning it was apparent that he wanted to talk to me, wanted, he said, to humanize his brother and help me see that while what Ricardo had done might be termed evil, Ricardo himself wasn't evil, merely sick. But Alberto wanted our meeting to take place at his home in Riverdale. "So that you can see that I'm not an inconsequential person," he explained.

I, on the other hand, wanted to interview him on my own turf—at my apartment, with my psychologist husband in a nearby room, or failing that, in a convivial, crowded restaurant. I'd been raised by a phobic mother, a woman so fearful that she never learned to drive, never traveled anywhere on her own, and who, when I went off to college, constantly deluged me with newspaper clippings about young women who'd been raped or otherwise brutalized. I'd long understood that there was a connection between those clippings and the things I wrote about, and that in part, I had chosen the work I had because I was attempting to counter the fears my mother had inculcated in me, fears that had limited and robbed her life and at various times seemed likely to do the same to my own. Yet I had remained a cautious person. And the fact of the matter was that I was afraid of being face-to-face with Alberto.

It wasn't only because his brother was a murderer. It was because, as I'd been reading in my husband's psychological tomes, psychopathy can run in families. But my desire to perform well at my work had always made me less timorous than I was naturally inclined to be. And so one morning when Alberto insisted yet again that I come to his home, I said all right.

Still, fear wasn't far from my mind on the day I rode up there. The address Alberto had given me was on a lovely, shady street, but the property was surrounded by a high wooden fence. Barricading oneself from one's neighbors is unusual in a friendly upper-middle-class community like Riverdale—I'd seen only one other fence as I'd driven through the neighborhood—and Alberto's need to cordon himself off worried me. Yet, propelled by my obsession with Ricardo, I opened a side gate Alberto had said he would leave unlatched and headed for the house. At once, my footsteps were greeted by a frenzied barking, and a large, ferocious-looking dog appeared in a front-room window.

It was too much for me. I turned to leave, and just then, Alberto opened his front door. "Come in, come in," he said, one hand on the dog's neck. "He won't hurt you."

Alberto was wearing jeans, a sweater, and a pair of white, shearling-lined house slippers. But more than the man, I was concentrating on the dog—a muscular dog with a broad head and powerful-looking jaws. "What is he?" I asked, standing rooted to my spot.

"A Staffordshire terrier."

"A *terrier*?"

I must have sounded as unbelieving as I felt, for
Alberto quickly came clean. "Pit bull. Staffordshire
terriers are pit bulls."

Why on earth does he need a pit bull? I wondered.
And perhaps that thought, too, communicated itself,
for Alberto said, "They're very good watchdogs, you
know. They bark like crazy when anyone approaches.
But they don't bite. At least this one doesn't."

"How come?"

"It's all in the training."

I was still standing stock-still. And I might have
remained that way except that at that moment a
slender, serene-looking woman came up alongside
Alberto and extended a hand to me. "I'm Kim
Caputo," she said in a voice as high and sweet as a
child's. "Won't you come in?" Behind her was a real
child, a ten-year-old boy in a baseball cap and shirt.
"Our son." Kim pushed him forward. "Matt."

"Truman," Matt said, shaking my hand. "The
dog's name is Truman."

"Truman Caputo—you get it?" Alberto smiled. It
was a quirky, hundred-watt smile—as dazzling as
Ricardo's must once have been, I told myself. Yet I
let the man and his wife, the boy and his dog, lead
me into the house. My thoughts of the sinister had
vanished. They'd been subsumed by the tableau
before my eyes, the sight of what I now saw—and
hoped I would continue to see—as being simply an
ordinary suburban family and its unlovely but loved
pet attempting to welcome a stranger.

I had told Alberto that what I was interested in
were his reminiscences about his and Ricardo's
childhood. I wanted to know who their parents
were, what their rearing had been, at what age
Ricardo had begun to seem violent or bizarre—if he
ever had. And I wanted to know details about the

events to which Kennedy had alluded in his sentencing-day speech and various press conferences: the beatings that Ricardo had suffered when he was a boy—had Alberto been beaten, too?—the rape he'd endured, his adolescent hospitalization.

Alberto had promised he could inform me about most of this, and as soon as I entered the house, I suggested we start our discussion. But the Caputos wanted to show me around. So we roamed through the house and I dutifully admired the dining room with its antique-reproduction table that Alberto had assembled and finished himself, the kitchen with its handsome china and pottery that Kim had collected, and the step-down study and rambling foyers lined with photographs taken by the many famous photographers whose pictures Alberto's company had developed.

Then at last, Alberto and Kim led me into the living room, a peaceful expanse dominated by a blue-and-white-tiled fireplace, and sat down opposite me. Matt, who had accompanied us on our tour of the house, sat down, too, an act that made Alberto frown. "We're going to be talking about Ricardo," he said gently to the boy, "so maybe you should go work on your computer."

Matt begged to stay, his face pouting like that of any ten-year-old being turned away from an adult cabal. But he was a well-brought-up child, mannerly and obliging, and after a few moments, he slipped away. When he did, I said, "He knows about Ricardo?"

"Everything," Kim replied in her sweet, high-toned voice. "We told him everything as soon as Ricardo turned up. We thought it would be best because it was all going to be on television, and if we hadn't told him, his friends might have."

"But although he knows about Ricardo," Alberto

interrupted, "we don't want him dwelling on it." He was startlingly handsome, short but wiry, with an oval face, suntanned complexion, high forehead, and arresting blue eyes.

I nodded at the soundness of the decision he was reporting to me and felt a moment's pity for him and Kim. It couldn't have been easy for them to tell their ten-year-old that his uncle was a practitioner and purveyor of slaughter.

I felt this burgeoning sympathy but I also felt edgy. When were we going to get started? So, producing my notebook, I said impatiently to Alberto, "Tell me about your parents." He leaned forward and shook his head, and for a moment I thought he'd changed his mind about talking to me. But a second later, as he again moved his head from side to side but this time smiled his winsome smile, I realized he was shaking his head at his memories, not at me. And indeed, soon afterward, he began talking, a stream of words cascading from his lips. "My parents? My parents? For years I hated them. Ricardo did, too. But now that I'm a father myself, I'm beginning to see that much of what I blamed them for were things they couldn't control or fix or do anything about. They were the products of their time, their place. No, the victims of those things."

As it turned out, I had opened a floodgate.

The story Alberto told me that afternoon reminded me of a Latin American novel. It was a story filled with mystery and religion, deep loves and tragic hates, cruel deceptions and hurtful betrayals, all set amid a background of paradisiacal islands, immense mountains, and desolate deserts.

It was into such a desert that Alberto and Ricardo's father, Alberto Matias Caputo, had made his way as a young man after leaving the cos-

mopolitan pleasures of Buenos Aires. Or being
forced to leave. Alberto Matias, who along with his
parents, brothers, and sisters had immigrated to
Argentina from Italy, was always close-mouthed
about why he had left the capital, traveled to the
foothills of the Andes, and taken up residence in the
provincial city of Mendoza, where the *zonda*, the
dry, disease-laden wind from the desert, swept regularly through streets of tightly shuttered houses.
Nor had Alberto Matias's siblings, who lived in
Buenos Aires, been inclined to offer much by way of
explanation to his elder son, Alberto, when, as an
adult, he sought them out. They had erected a wall
of silence around their connection to their brother
Alberto Matias, who, once having parted from
them, kept his distance and established a life for
himself in Mendoza that gave him connections he
apparently preferred to those of family life.

He had women, lots of them; friends, many of
them on the local police force; and employees,
workers in the small construction business he
established and turned into so much of a success
that he could spend his evenings doing what he
loved best, drinking and gambling beneath the art
deco chandeliers in the casino of Mendoza's principal hotel. A handsome man with slicked-back hair
and a dark, brooding expression, he had *estampa*,
the aristocratic bearing much admired by
Argentinians. And although he was not wealthy, he
loved the trappings of wealth—fine clothes, good
horses. Partying, he wore expensive long-jacketed
suits similar to those of his hero, Juan Perón; playing polo, he sported jodhpurs, high boots, silk
ascots around his neck. He was also, not unlike his
son Alberto, a talker, a spinner of tales who could
entertain a group of cronies for hours, and not
unlike his son Ricardo, he was given to deceit or at

least exaggeration—"he was a con artist," Alberto characterized him at one point.

Alberto's mother, his and Ricardo's, was much younger than Alberto Matias. She was seventeen years old when she met him, and he was in his forties. Curly-haired and fair-skinned, but with deep-set eyes and high cheekbones, Alicia was descended from a long line of Spaniards, the adventurers, soldiers, and settlers who had overrun the native populations of Argentina, but her exotic face hinted at a distant mingling of the blood of the *colonos* with those of the people they had conquered.

Long residence in Argentina had not brought Alicia's people riches. They were country folk, plagued by poverty and ignorance. Alicia's father was a gaucho, a laborer who took care of horses on an island ranch; her mother was a homemaker and child-rearer—she had nine children, five girls and four boys. Few of them received more than a paltry education. Alicia was sent to a distant convent school until she was twelve, but after that her education ceased. Still, she enjoyed the boons as well as the hardships of country life, growing up enthralled by the heavy scents of flowers and animal breath that wafted through the green fields of the ranch, the raucous cries of the birds overhead, the brilliant colors of the swift-moving river that flowed past the island. "She used to tell us she grew up in paradise," Alberto said.

Paradise ended for her soon after she met Alberto Matias. She was introduced to him by an older sister who took her to his house in Mendoza and, promising she would be right back, disappeared. Perhaps the introduction was undertaken casually. Or perhaps it was part of a plan. Alicia was at the time engaged to marry a young man who was as poor as herself, and her sister may have been trying to show her that there was more to the world of men than she realized. Or her sister may even have been cool-heartedly hoping that her exotic-looking younger sister might be made to help their poverty-stricken family by catching the fancy of the well-to-do Alberto Matias. Whatever, she left her little sister in his home, went away, and failed for days to return. By the time she did, Alberto Matias had seduced Alicia.

It wasn't difficult. The young country girl had been awed by Alberto Matias's comfortable home, a house with fine furnishings and discreet servants. And she had felt honored by the attentions of her host, a man so much more polished, educated, and well-off than any she'd known before. When he told her he adored her, she was flattered and pleased and gave herself to him with a joyous heart.

Three months later, the couple married. The aging, debonair bachelor had fallen in love with Alicia, or so she would later tell her children, allowing that it was a miracle and a mystery since she was so unsophisticated that she had never, as she used to put it, "been to the center of Buenos Aires, never even owned a bathing suit." She would also tell her children that she wasn't pregnant when she and Alberto Matias married, but that because she was a minor and was lacking her parents' consent, Alberto Matias persuaded the local authorities to let him marry her by telling them that she was.

Theirs was a civil wedding. Alberto Matias refused to be married by a priest, a scorning of propriety that deeply troubled his religious young bride. And in the next few months her troubles mounted. Alberto Matias had married her, but he had no intention, she discovered, of giving up the pleasures that had filled his life as a single man. At night, if he hadn't invited his cronies to the house to play cards, he went out to the casino and afterward to the *cabarateras*, where he would pick up women. When she learned this, Alicia was frightened that he would catch a venereal disease and pass it on to her. But most of all, she was humiliated, for frequently he came home with one of his women and said, "This is a friend of mine and I want you to put her up."

She never refused. He had a terrible temper. Daily, he would rail at her, and also at God and the Virgin Mary, which bothered her just as much. And on several occasions, he struck her.

She had, by the time the beatings began, given birth to their first child, Alberto. And she had even succeeded in getting Alberto Matias married to her in the bosom of the Church. She had done it without his knowledge. He had become ill with typhus and was lying in a hospital, at death's open door. Alicia had begged a priest to give him last rites and, while he was at it, to marry them, even though her husband was in a coma.

Alberto Matias had recovered, and to her amazement, he hadn't been angry with her. "Perhaps you and your God saved my life," he had told her. But the marriage, even once she had made it legitimate in the eyes of God, remained a misery to her, for her husband remained a reprobate.

Still, she bore him another child, their second son, Ricardo. And she tried to love Alberto Matias, always praying to Jesus and the Virgin to give her strength to bear with his harsh and errant ways. And with her loneliness. It was a loneliness so deep it seemed like the river that had surrounded her childhood home, and sometimes she feared she might drown in it.

Then fate, or her prayers, rescued her. She made a friend, a roomer whom Alberto Matias had hired to do domestic chores. Luis Pinto, who worked in

Alberto Matias's factory, was a provincial, just like Alicia. And in this, as in many other ways, he was altogether different from Alberto Matias. He was young, a year or two younger than Alicia. He was helpful, always assisting her with the children. He was respectful, always addressing her calmly and gently. And instead of running from her, he confided in her, told her his dreams and his longings. One day, her loneliness evaporating at the mere sound of his voice, she went to bed with Luis.

She wasn't sorry. Not then, nor for many years afterward. She and Luis were in love.

They saw each other secretly over the next year, and their love grew like the *parras* on the hillside. And then Alicia became pregnant again.

She could have kept her indiscretion a secret, borne and birthed the child and let Alberto Matias assume it was his. But such a subterfuge seemed wicked to her. Soon after she gave birth—this time, she had a daughter, little Alicia—she told her husband about her affair and about the baby's uncertain parentage. *"Puta!"* he bellowed, and threw her out of the house. Her, and little Alicia, too. But he wouldn't let her take the boys. The boys were his, he told her, and he wasn't going to let them be raised by a whore.

Alicia left. But afterward she came back, begging for custody of the boys, and when Alberto Matias refused, she began going to the house regularly and begging to be allowed just to see them. But each time, Alberto Matias denied her entry, and not once did he tell her sons that she wanted them or even that she had tried to visit them. "She abandoned you," he said whenever her name came up. "The whore."

Alberto didn't miss her very much. He was seven, already in school and busy with friends. It was dif-

ferent for Ricardo. Five and a half, and a difficult
child, he often got on the wrong side of Alberto
Matias, who was far less gentle with him than his
mother had been. When he wet his bed, which he
couldn't seem to stop doing, his father would grab
his mattress, toss it out the door, and make him
sleep on it outside. And when he cried, which he
often did, Alberto Matias would throw him down
onto his bed, once flinging him down so hard that
the bed broke.

But in other ways, Alberto Matias was permis-
sive, or at least so inattentive that his sons could do
things that were prohibited to other boys in the
neighborhood. They drank *café con leche,* sucking it
in from a big, nippled mayonnaise jar—Alberto
remembers sucking at the jar until he was eleven.
And they could fondle the maids—Alberto remembers doing this at the age of nine, and seeing
Ricardo do it when he was seven.

There was something else Ricardo liked to do at
that age. He liked playing a game that Alberto had
invented, a game about forts and troops and soldiers they called *tefuer,* which was *fuerte*—fort—
spelled inside out. In the game, they had guns,
chased after people, spied on them. Alberto was
always the commander, and Ricardo the follower,
but he didn't mind. *"Juguemos al tefuer,"* he would
say each morning, "Let's play *tefuer,"* and Alberto
would set a story in motion, some plot in which they
had to sneak over a wall, storm a barricade, run for
their lives. But Ricardo always wanted Alberto to
put girls into the plot. He wanted them to chase
girls, capture them, rape them. *"Las cojamos,"* he'd
say, using the Mendoza word for sexual intercourse.
Las cojamos. Let's fuck them.

"It was puzzling," Alberto said to me. "It wasn't
something I particularly wanted in the game. But

Ricardo loved it. And as he hated two little girls who lived across the way from us, I put them into the game, and we'd pretend we were going after them. We did this over and over again, and I got bored with it, but Ricardo could never get enough of it. And to this day, it haunts me—I mean, did my imagination have anything to do with arousing the images that would later come to *be* Ricardo's life?"

Alberto felt a goodly amount of guilt about Ricardo, a guilt arising not so much from their childhood games as from the fact that Ricardo had turned into a murderer while he himself had become a successful businessman. He kept wrestling with the difference between them and wondering why, given their same parentage and rearing, Ricardo had collapsed under the weight of their history. "I just don't get it," he said at one point. "I mean, Ricardo and I suffered terribly as children. And we had the *same* sufferings. But I'm not a killer. Except in business. Where it's okay."

I laughed, and he went on, "We suffered because our father was so harsh and because we had no mother. And then our story gets even worse. When I was eleven and Ricardo was nine, our father died and our mother came back and claimed us. And after that we were poor, dirt poor. Our mother had nothing. We hated that. We hated *her*. Because our father had brainwashed us against her. Against her and Luis, whom she married right away and who right away began bossing us around and telling us what to do."

"Was Luis brutal?" I asked. Kennedy, in attempting to create sympathy for Ricardo, had made a point of saying in his press conferences that Ricardo had been beaten by his stepfather.

"Well, he beat us when we disobeyed. But that was the way men in that time and place disciplined their children. All the boys we knew had fathers who beat them, and they didn't become killers."

"So what *do* you think made Ricardo a killer?"

Alberto put his head in his hands. "I don't really know. I just know that starting at a very early age, he was different from other little boys."

"Different how?"

"Well, he was always telling lies. I mean, I told lies, too. But I always knew what was real and what was a lie. With him, you couldn't be sure. He seemed to believe his lies."

"What else was different?"

"The way he fought. Fighting was nothing in and of itself. The boys we hung out with beat up on each other all the time. But when Ricardo got into a fight, there was something savage about him. Something that struck me, even then, as too intense. I don't know. Maybe he got a head injury that time my father threw him down onto his bed. Or maybe it was because of that time he says he was raped."

"When was the rape?"

"When we were still living with my father. Ricardo says that one of the maids sent him out to buy bread and on his way home a man who lived near the bakery sodomized him. But I'm not sure it ever really happened. The first I heard of it was when Ricardo turned himself in, and he could have been making it up to make people pity him. As I said, Ricardo's relationship to the truth has never been a particularly strong one."

I was struck by the skepticism in Alberto's voice. For a man who had insisted he wanted to humanize his brother, which I had taken to mean that he wanted to show him in a good light, so far he had told me nothing admirable about Ricardo. Perhaps there was nothing. "Do you like your brother?" I asked.

"He's my brother."

"Yes, but aside from that."

"He's a sick person. He was sick from childhood. He didn't have friends. He got on the bad side of teachers. I remember that at one point, my mother and Luis had to take him out of the school we were going to and send him to a religious boarding school. We packed this big trunk for him, but the next thing I knew, he was back. I guess the school sent him back."

"Why?"

"Who knows? My mother and Luis didn't talk about it. And whatever Ricardo said, I probably didn't believe. Because as I told you, he was always lying. I remember that when he was eleven, he ran away from home for two days, and when the police found him on the street, he said he'd been kidnapped. Nobody believed him. You couldn't take him seriously. For example, there was this time that Luis took us to a friend's ranch to go shooting, and the man who owned the ranch had a ram tied up there. Ricardo began taunting the animal, challenging it to butt him, but when he was reprimanded, he said that he hadn't been doing it—even though everyone had seen him."

I nodded. The portrait of Ricardo as a boy that was emerging reminded me of a page I'd often had occasion to refer to in *DSM-IV*, the diagnostic manual used by the majority of American psychiatrists. A patient, the manual directs, may be diagnosed as having an antisocial personality disorder—that is, as being a psychopath or sociopath—if his history reveals three or more of such behaviors as playing truant, running away from home, being cruel to animals, telling frequent lies, or initiating frequent physical fights "before the age of fifteen." Ricardo, before the age of fifteen, indeed before the age of thirteen, had exhibited most of these behaviors. And after that? "Tell me about your adolescence," I said to Alberto.

He leaned back, arms crossed over his head. "Our adolescence," he mused. "Our adolescence. I'm not sure I can make you understand it unless I tell you what Argentina was like then."

The Argentina he proceeded to tell me about, the Argentina in which both he and Ricardo entered their young manhood, was a country torn by political violence. In 1963, when Ricardo was fourteen and Alberto sixteen, an elected president was overthrown by the military and a dictator placed in control of the government. This was nothing new for Argentina, which ever since 1930 had experienced one military coup after another, the most famous of which exiled the populist president Juan Perón and forbade the public mention of either the deposed leader or his wife, Evita. Nor would the military's penchant for taking over elected governments end soon. In the late 1970s it would produce one of the cruelest regimes in twentieth-century history, that of the junta that "disappeared" thousands of its own citizens in the infamous Dirty War. When Alberto and Ricardo were teenagers, that harsh government was in the future, but the seeds of its rule by torture and murder, guns and bombs, were already present in the regime that came to power in their youth.

That regime banned labor unions, political parties, and even Eastern philosophy. It dissolved the country's congress and its supreme court. And it sparked terrorist activity on both the left and the right. "Everyone, all the kids we knew, had guns," Alberto said. "And everyone was antiauthority. Because the government was so terrible."

During high school, Alberto joined a secret right-wing organization. "You had to do things to be accepted," he explained. "Things with guns and bombs at night. But I had friends in left-wing groups that were also committed to political violence. Politics dominated the lives of all my friends. But not Ricardo's life. He and *his* friends had guns, too, but his friends were all *ratóns*, rats who weren't the least bit interested in politics or ideas."

Ricardo's primary interest, according to Alberto, was money. And in the atmosphere of violence that permeated Argentina, he and his friends, armed and daring, began obtaining money by petty thefts.

Interestingly, Ricardo had also by then mastered another technique for getting money, one he would rely on the rest of his life. He extracted it from women, primarily foreigners to Mendoza who had come to see its mountains and vineyards. Hanging out at the cafés and discos where newcomers congregated, he would pick up female tourists, go to bed with them, and subsequently ask them for a little cash.

"Women felt sorry for him," Alberto said. "He was so cute and so sexy—and so poor. They'd help him out."

There was no dearth of sympathetic women. "He was so successful at finding women that it used to bother me," Alberto went on. "I mean, I was the older brother, but he had many more sexual experiences than I did. I didn't understand it when we were young. I thought he must be smarter than me. But now I can see his appeal. He came on so helpless, and women loved his helplessness."

Did he steal from those women? Or just badger them for handouts? "I think he just borrowed money," Alberto said. "And then didn't pay it back. I met my first girlfriend because she went out with

Ricardo and loaned him some money and then didn't hear from him again. She kept phoning and phoning the house to try to get hold of him and get her money back, and finally I invited her over and we started going together."

However Ricardo got his money, he used it for luxuries. Alberto recalled that he sometimes borrowed Ricardo's clothes because they were better than his own. "He had fancy shoes. Great jackets. Things that made him look rich, even though we were living in poverty. In Argentina, we call someone like that a *fanfarrón*, a person who's a bluffer, who lives, say, in a one-room apartment but drives a Mercedes. Ricardo became a *fanfarrón*—maybe he wanted to look the way he might have looked if we'd grown up with our father."

Ricardo's pursuit of money continued throughout his adolescence. Alberto had no recollection of Ricardo's having entered a psychiatric hospital when he was sixteen. "It must have been when I went to school in Buenos Aires for a time," Alberto said. But he remembered a different kind of confinement. When Ricardo was seventeen, he was briefly jailed for a robbery, and Alberto was delegated by their parents to go down to the town jail and get him out.

By then, Ricardo's relationship with his mother and stepfather, who had gone on to have two more daughters, was in tatters. And soon he left home altogether. He'd found work as a door-to-door cosmetics salesman, he told his family, and would be traveling all over the country. After that he rarely returned to Mendoza, although on the few occasions he did, he always brought with him expensive presents.

"My poor brother," Alberto said as he reminisced about the old days. "From his youth, he was always in love with money. And one night after we first came to the United States and he was working as a waiter, I remember him lying on his bed and posing for a picture—naked except for a great scattering of dollar bills he'd gotten as tips."

It was growing late. Matt came in and asked Alberto if he could help him with a computer problem. Kim came in and said she was making supper and when did Alberto think he'd be ready to eat? "I guess we'd better wind it up," Alberto said to me, "though it's too bad. I like talking to you. It's sort of like talking to a therapist."

"Well, hardly," I demurred. His flattery had discomfited me.

"No, no. It is. It makes me think about things I haven't thought about for years. See them in a different perspective. In fact, why don't you come back another time? I could show you the videotapes."

"What videotapes?"

"Dr. Park Dietz's interviews with Ricardo. Kennedy gave them to me and I haven't been able to bring myself to watch them. Would you want to see them?"

Would I want to? I'd felt all afternoon as I'd listened to Alberto that although I was beginning to know Ricardo, he was still a distant figure, a shadow cloaked in history and family mythology. The idea of watching him as he was today, of hearing him explain himself to a psychiatrist, was immensely attractive to me, so attractive that I felt some need to mask my eagerness. "Yeah, might be interesting," I muttered.

Alberto smiled that dazzling smile of his. He had seen right through me. "Next week. Come back next week."

I wished he wasn't quite so appealing. His very helpfulness made me uneasy, made me think of Ricardo's famed ability to enchant and seduce.

Ricardo had used that ability to pursue ulterior motives. Could Alberto have some ulterior motive in being so seductive with me?

If so, I couldn't think what it might be beyond the obvious one, the desire to have me portray him and his family in as good a light as possible. And the more I tried to conjure up some more unsavory intention, the less I was able to. Alberto did indeed have the selfsame kind of charm Ricardo was reputed to have had, but as far as I could determine, it wasn't in the service of some nefarious end but of some almost automatic wish to please and be liked. Most likely it was a family characteristic, I told myself, a product of the genes inherited from the dashing Alberto Matias.

I said yes, next week.

13

The tapes, when I watched them with Alberto some days later, proved mesmerizing. Dr. Park Elliott Dietz was one of America's foremost forensic psychiatrists. Hearing him question Ricardo not only about his murders but also about his childhood memories and intimate sexual fantasies was, for someone like myself who fancies herself a scholar of the psychology of criminal behavior, as exciting as listening to a master class taught by a virtuoso. Dietz, whose boyish face and deep-set, owlish eyes were familiar to me from television, never appeared on the screen—the camera was focused exclusively on Ricardo—but I felt his presence. It was there in his gentle, soothing voice, his insightful questions, the subtlety with which he teased out the information that could help him determine Ricardo's mental status.

He began his examination by informing Ricardo that he had come to ascertain the truth about that status, but he made no bones about his dedication to objectivity. "If the truth helps you," he said, "I'll tell it. But if it doesn't, I'll still tell the truth." Then he asked Ricardo to tell him about his childhood.

"My mother left my brother and me for another

man," Ricardo said, and at once began to talk about himself in words full of self-pity. "I was left in the care of maids. I was beaten by my father. Then, my mother came back. But I was very much rejected by her."

Dietz kept him talking, listened to him ventilate his anger at his mother: "When she went away, I was raped, I was bleeding, and she wasn't there"; his rage at his stepfather: "He beat me, too, and later he made me pay for my room and board"; his wrath at the priests who had educated him: "They slapped you, slapped you hard, if you got in trouble"; and his fury at the doctors who had cared for him when he had hospitalized himself as a teenager: "They said they'd help me, but they didn't, they studied me, treated me like a guinea pig." And soon, Dietz began firing questions about those teenage years at Ricardo.

"When you were a boy, did you ever force yourself on a girl? Or another boy?" he asked.

"No," Ricardo said indignantly. But he followed his denial by offering up the information that he had begun masturbating at the age of ten or eleven, as if that activity at what he seemed to consider a precocious age might indicate some tendency toward mental illness.

Dietz pursued the direction into which Ricardo's thoughts had taken him. "What did you think about when masturbating?" he asked.

"Fornicating," Ricardo said, providing nothing out of the ordinary. "And parts of a woman. Breasts and pelvis."

"Did you ever use pictures to masturbate?"

"Yes, from magazines."

"What were your favorites?"

"A woman sitting down with a bathing suit on. I used that all the time. The breasts were showing. They made me feel very excited."

Dietz probed further, no doubt trying to see if Ricardo had ever entertained the kinds of sadistic or fetishistic obsessions that were the hallmark of orgasm-driven serial murderers. "Did anything else about the picture excite you? Anything about the hair or jewelry or shoes?"

But Ricardo said, "No. Breasts excited me. And eyes excited me."

"What about clothing?" Dietz persisted.

"Yeah. Underwear. Black, soft underwear."

"Did you ever buy underwear for a woman?" Dietz asked next.

"Yeah. For Natalie," Ricardo said.

"Would she wear it for you?"

"Yeah."

"Did you find other things useful as toys during sex? Handcuffs? Ropes? Gags? Leather or whips? Rubber or vinyl?"

"No." Ricardo sounded uneasy and amplified his answer by saying, "With Natalie, it was just plain sex."

"What about with other women?" Dietz pressed him.

But Ricardo's responses continued to be within the range of normality. "Before Natalie, I went out with prostitutes and it was just regular paying and coming inside them."

Having failed to elicit youthful sexual deviancy, Dietz moved to another line of questioning—a line that might establish psychopathy. "Did you use drugs before the age of fifteen?" he asked blandly.

"No." Then: "Well, only marijuana."

"Did you drink alcohol before the age of fifteen?"

"Yeah."

"Did you get into trouble?"

Ricardo seemed more comfortable with this line of questioning, little recognizing that his answers to

Dietz's nonsexual queries were as potentially damning to him as any answers he might have given to the sexual ones. "Yeah. My stepfather and my mother threw me out of the house when I came home drunk. I was around thirteen."

"What was the first time you left home and stayed away overnight?"

"It was right after I was finished at the priest school."

"Why were you thrown out?"

"My family didn't like me. Luis, especially. He thought I was no good. He used to tell my mother I was crazy."

"Did you ever become violent to Luis?"

"I was afraid of him physically. But I told him to fuck off. And I dreamed about killing him. About making him suffer."

"What other things did you do before the age of fifteen?" Dietz asked, his tranquil voice giving no sign of the significance of what he had been finding out.

"Nothing. I never did anything to anybody. I just had fantasies. And sometimes I said crazy things."

"What kinds of crazy things?"

"What I felt, and what the world was all about."

"What did you think the world was all about?"

"I thought it was mean and cruel."

"Who was your best friend?"

Ricardo's answer was like a classical illustration of the psychopath's notorious detachment from other people. "Myself," he answered unwittingly.

Alberto and I watched the tapes for hours. The camera never shifted from Ricardo's face, a brooding face with thin lips that didn't smile and dark-circled eyes that didn't blink. The face seemed almost to inhabit a corner of Alberto's study, for it hovered in his extra-large videoscreen like some looming domestic icon. And what was strange was that even when it described stabbings and beatings, the screams of victims and the directives of imagined spirits, it remained expressionless.

These descriptions were curiously antiseptic. Ricardo claimed to remember little of his actual actions when he committed murder, remembered chiefly that each time, just before he killed, he saw colors and dots and lines in front of his eyes or heard growling voices in his mind's ear. "They didn't say to kill. But they said, 'Blood,' and, 'We want your blood.'"

When he killed bank teller Natalie Brown, he told Dr. Dietz, "I can't remember picking up the knife. Or striking her. I heard screams. But they were kind of far away. Behind the lines."

When he killed psychologist Judith Becker, "I saw the colors. And I heard screams. But I remember nothing else."

When he killed film editor Barbara Taylor, "I saw the colors again, and then I was looking at her hair, and I grabbed her throat."

When he killed graduate student Laura Gomez, "we were sitting together and talking and all of a sudden I saw the colors and dots and I hit her with an object I had in my hand. I think it was an iron bar."

Ricardo also provided Dietz, albeit in a guarded way, with further information about his sexual interactions with some of the women he had admitted killing. Natalie, he said, had had lots of men before him, but considered him the best of the lot. Barbara, he said, liked to make love after smoking pot. Judith, he claimed, was sexually kinky. "She would ask me, 'Ricardo, why don't you do something? Slap me. Go in from the back. Pose with a knife in your hand.' When I did those things, she would start fingering herself. And she'd have an orgasm."

"What other things did she ask you to do?"

"She asked me to push her onto the bed. To push her and slap her and make love from the back."

"Did she ever ask you to tie her up?"

"Yes. With nylon panty hose."

"Anything else?"

"*She* had leather. Short leather skirts that she used to wear during making love."

"Did she have leather straps for tying up?"

"No."

"Did she have a dildo?"

"I think so."

"Did she ever ask you to use it?"

"No." Then Ricardo hesitated, perhaps trying to ascertain what the best answer to that question might be, and suddenly he changed his mind. "Yes. Yes, once."

Ricardo also provided Dietz with information about his interactions with the women immediately before he killed them, information that invariably served to present him rather than the women as having been victimized. Natalie, he said, had been pressuring him to get married, even though she knew he was feeling depressed. "We went upstairs and made love. It was short sex. I don't even remember if I ejaculated. I got on top of her and I came off. And she asked me what was wrong. And she asked me about marriage. [But] I was feeling like in a daze. I was depressed. And I felt angry because I felt helpless."

Laura, too, he said, had talked marriage to him at an unfortunate moment, a time when he couldn't "take the responsibility. So I felt a huge depression. And I heard the voices again."

Barbara, he said, had plied him with drugs just before he killed her because she wanted more sex from him than he was able to provide. "We had been making love and smoking marijuana all night. And then, I couldn't get my sex erected anymore. She said she would give me a pill. I think it was speed. I don't know if it was the pill or me, Doctor, but I saw the colors again."

But it was Judith, who had once inspired him to write love poetry, who came in for the harshest blame. Not only did she want nothing but sex from him, Ricardo said, but the sex she wanted, particularly just before he killed her, was abhorrent to him. "I went to her house and right away she wanted to make love. She took her clothes off. She kissed me on the penis. And masturbated me. Then she asked me to do the real part—insert my penis into her anus. She had an orgasm while I was in her anus. Then she wanted the vagina. She didn't ask me to wash in between." He further insisted, somewhat stuffily, "I didn't want to do it. I think it's unhealthy."

I'd never believed that Judith had asked Ricardo to make love to her anally; I'd thought it more likely that he himself had demanded the act of Judith—and not because I didn't believe that some women enjoy anal sex. My conviction had sprung from the fact that, in Judith's case, Ricardo's claim that she had had a taste for pain and fear in bed had also been hard to believe. More recently, my conviction had been reinforced by a passage I'd read in V. S. Naipaul's insightful study of Argentina, *The Return of Eva Perón*: "The act of straight sex, easily bought, is of no great consequence to the [Argentine] macho. His conquest of a woman is complete only when he has buggered her. This is what the woman has it in her power to deny; this is what the brothel game is all about, the passionless Latin adventure that begins with talk of *amor*. *La tuve en el culo*, I've had her in the arse: this is how the macho reports victory to his circle, or dismisses a desertion. Contemporary sexologists give a general dispensation to buggery. But the buggering of women is of special significance in Argentina and other Latin American countries. The Church considers it a heavy sin, and prostitutes hold it in horror. By imposing on her what prostitutes reject, and what he knows to be a kind of sexual black mass, the Argentine macho, in the main of Spanish or Italian peasant ancestry, consciously dishonors his victim."

I remembered this passage as I listened to Ricardo talk about Judith's final sexual demand and I was awestruck by the man's insatiable need to present himself as a victim, a dishonored victim. Had Dietz recognized this? From his calm voice on the videotape, there was no way of telling. But it didn't matter. In the end, he had, of course, come to the conclusion that Ricardo's view of himself as a victim not just of women but of mental illness wasn't valid.

The whole while Dietz had been asking his questions and Ricardo had been giving his answers, Alberto, sitting alongside me on a small couch with Truman curled at our feet, had kept stopping the tape with his remote to proffer observations. When Ricardo talked about Natalie's wanting to marry him, he said, "He's lying. I think every time he was rejected by a woman, he killed her. But he always makes it sound as if he was rejecting them." When Ricardo talked about his isolation as a child, Alberto said, "You know, I think the prosecutors may be right that he's malingering. He remembers all sorts of little details, but not the big things, as if he'd planned certain parts of his story." And when Ricardo mentioned to Dietz that he was contem-

plating suicide and had no qualms about doing
away with himself because he didn't believe the soul
lived on after death, Alberto blurted out, "This really gets me! Because Ricardo's been asking me for
Bibles and saying he's religious, and I've been telling
him that no matter what he's done, it's not too late
to square himself with God." He spoke so sharply
that Truman stirred from his nap and gave a low,
sleepy growl. "I've been talking to Ricardo like I'm a
priest or something," Alberto went on indignantly.
"But maybe he isn't religious. Maybe he's been lying
about that, too."

I felt that the tapes were opening Alberto's eyes,
giving him a new view of his brother, or at least
allowing him to express a view that he had long held
but, out of family loyalty, denied, even to himself.
Indeed, I was certain that although he had initially
agreed to speak with me because he'd wanted me to
see Ricardo as he claimed to see him, as someone ill
rather than evil, what was happening was that as a
result of watching the tapes, he was coming around
to my view—that Ricardo was a manipulator.

This certainty grew when, after we finished
watching the tapes, Alberto rose and, pulling open
the drapes that masked the windows in the TV
room, said, "I wish I knew the real reason Ricardo
turned himself in. He says it's because of remorse,
but somehow, I don't believe him."

"Why not?" I asked as the previously darkened
room flooded with late-afternoon sunlight.

"I don't know. But when his wife was here doing
that *PrimeTime Live* show, she told me that the med-
ical-supplies people Ricardo was working for in
Mexico were like the Mafia down there. Then he
decided to go into business for himself, and his
bosses got very mad. And that's when he disappeared."

"And turned up in Argentina," I exclaimed.

Alberto nodded.

"So he *had* to flee Mexico," I said triumphantly. In *my* mind's ear I was hearing, as clearly as Ricardo claimed to hear voices, the raspy sound of John McGrath, Gordon McEwan's partner, saying to me so many months ago, "People don't come down with remorse like a flu or head cold. There's got to be more to the story." And in my mind's eye, I could picture Elise McCarthy sitting opposite me and sliding across her scarred table the article from *Clarín* about Ricardo's abrupt escape from Mexican police who were supposedly attempting to shake him down for money.

"Do you know about the article in *Clarín?*" I asked Alberto and when he shook his head, I told him about it. "The newspaper reported that Ricardo had told somebody or other that he had to bribe his way out of Mexico."

"Who was it?"

"I don't know. I thought maybe you'd be able to tell me."

Alberto frowned. "I didn't know anything about Ricardo, hadn't heard a word from or about him for twenty years until my parents called me from Mendoza, said he was there, and put him on the phone."

"Maybe your parents know the reason. Did you ask them?"

"No. It was all so chaotic. I'd just returned from a trip to Mexico, a trip where I'd been very close to the town Ricardo was living in. And when Ricardo got on the phone and told me where he'd been living and what he'd done, I was terrified the police would think I had seen him down there, which I hadn't, and all I could think about was my own skin. I wanted him to just go away again, disappear. But anyway, by the time he called, he'd been home for a few weeks and he was already saying this stuff about being so religious and wanting to surrender himself in order to atone."

"So you found him a lawyer?"

"Yes. Kennedy. I got to him through Hamilton Fish, who'd run for political office up here and was a friend of mine. I did it because my parents asked me to—they'd already taken Ricardo to an Argentinian lawyer, but he'd said an American attorney would be necessary."

"What did you tell Kennedy?"

"What Ricardo told me to tell him. That he was nuts, that he'd killed those women because he heard voices, and that he wanted to turn himself in because he was suffering from remorse. But it could have been a story he concocted after he went home and saw my parents. I mean, when he showed up at home, he said he wanted to turn himself in. But he wavered, too, talked sometimes about getting my parents to hide him. They refused. My mother said he had to make his peace with God. And maybe she filled his head with all that atonement stuff and he thought it would fly, get him off or at least into a mental hospital, not a prison."

I was surprised by how cynical Alberto was sounding about his brother. "You think he was scheming," I pointed out, "yet you stood by him, got Kim to write that press release about his having hallucinations and being sick?"

"I believed it then," Alberto, who had begun putting away the videotapes, said simply. "There's been a lot of water under the bridge since then. Like this stuff about Mexico."

I sighed. "I wish I could track it down. Do you suppose Ricardo's wife would speak to me?"

Alberto shook his head. "She's scared of Ricardo.

But maybe if you went down to Argentina, you could find out something about it. Find out who gave that information to *Clarín*."

The thought had crossed my mind many times. But I'd made no plans to go. Now, however, I was experiencing a surge of enthusiasm for such an expedition. "Your mother," I said, "how extraordinary that she would talk her own son into turning himself in. Do you think that if I went down there, she'd speak with me?"

Alberto was struggling to get a particularly recalcitrant tape into its jacket. "I imagine so," he replied distractedly.

"But why?" I said, as much to myself as to him.

"Because for one thing, the local media picked up on Ricardo's having called her a whore. She was very upset about that, along with everything else, and she might want to talk to someone who'd set that particular record straight."

"You'd ask her to?" I persisted.

"Sure."

"But why?" I said again. And then what was really on my mind tumbled out. "In fact, why the hell are you being so helpful to me?"

"Because I want you to find out the truth about why Ricardo turned himself in." Alberto shoved the tapes into a cabinet and slammed the door. "Because I want to know if he's been bullshitting me all these months."

"Well, maybe I'll go," I said then, tentatively. "Maybe I'll try to talk to that lawyer Ricardo saw down there. And the psychiatrist he visited."

I had no idea if they would agree to meet with me. But the idea of going to Argentina had taken hold of my imagination. Argentina. The bottom of the world. "Who else do you suppose I could see if I go down to Argentina?"

"There's that psychiatrist Ricardo saw when he was a teenager. I don't know him, but I think he's been talking to the press."

"Good idea." I was speaking firmly now. My idle daydream of going to Argentina was becoming a resolution, a plan.

14

I flew to Argentina in June 1995. It was fifteen months since Ricardo had turned himself in, ten years since Gordon McEwan had first uttered his name to me. On the plane to Buenos Aires, an overnight flight, I dreamed that Ricardo was sitting across the aisle, sitting so close that if I reached out my arm, I might grasp him. Or he me. It was a nightmare and I was glad to awaken from it to the twinkling lights of Buenos Aires, mile upon mile of them piercing the still-black sky of what was, down below, a windy autumnal dawn.

The airport was chaotic. I'd been warned by a friend of a friend, an Argentinian psychiatrist with whom I was planning to meet later in the day, not to take a taxi to my hotel, but to take a special airport-to-city limousine instead. "Never never an airport taxicab!" he'd faxed me. "They are unreliable." But so was the limousine service he'd recommended. I joined a milling throng around the service's desk, put my name down for a vehicle, then was told I'd have to wait at least an hour and maybe more before one became available. I cooled my heels awhile, watching battalions of departing passengers stampede toward a luggage-wrapping station.

(Argentinians don't trust even diligently locked suit-cases to their baggage handlers, but pay several dol-lars a case to get their bags sealed into formfitting, airtight plastic, rather as if they were like super-market chickens.) Then, too exhausted from the long night's ride to wait any longer for a private con-veyance, I boarded a bus whose driver had been shouting that he was going from the international airport at which I had landed to the one used for domestic travel and that he would be stopping en route in the heart of downtown Buenos Aires. I was ecstatic to learn about that bus, not just because taking it meant I'd soon be getting to my hotel room and having the luxury of a shower and a nap in a horizontal position, but because I'd understood the driver. My Spanish was coming back.

The sun, a cold sun unlike the hot early-summer one that had been shining when I'd left New York the day before, was up by now, and as we bumped and shimmied through the outskirts of Argentina's capital, I had a chance to examine my surround-ings: flat fields, oddly shaped trees, paper-strewn roadsides, run-down houses, and cars that looked as if they'd been assembled for a period movie, big rounded American cars from the forties and tiny Beetle-like German cars from the fifties, many of them with stripped paint and wrecked bodies. Argentina, it seemed to me in the first hour of my visit there, was stuck in a time warp, was a place where the past was more in evidence than the pre-sent, or at least more in evidence than what we in North America consider the present.

I had the same impression when the bus finally entered the capital. Here, there were office build-ings and crowds of people on their way to work. But the office buildings were shabby and squat, and the people were dressed in clothes that had long ago

gone out of style up north. It was as if I'd gone back
in time, not just back to a chilly season I'd already
experienced, but back to decades I'd already lived
through.

That afternoon, after registering at my hotel and
getting my shower and nap, I toured the city. I saw
more elegant buildings than I'd seen earlier, vestiges
not of decades but of centuries past, patioed eigh-
teenth-century houses, ornate nineteenth-century
palaces. I saw the colorful bohemian section of
Palermo, the busy shopping district of Florida, and
the affluent neighborhood of Recoleta with its
amazing cemetery, a necropolis where the tombs
look like mansions. (In one of them, I was informed,
Evita Perón lies buried, her bones so far beneath the
ground that her body, which was once stolen by her
enemies, is thoroughly safe from disinterment.)
Later, I went to a concert at the Teatro Colón, one of
the most exquisite opera houses in the world, with
Dr. David Rosenfeld, the psychiatrist friend of my
friend. I had written to Rosenfeld, asking for his
help in trying to set up interviews with the psychiatrists who had treated Ricardo, and Rosenfeld had
come through, had provided me with a contact in
Mendoza who knew many of the psychiatrists there.

Rosenfeld was a psychoanalyst. He hadn't known
Ricardo, but he knew about his case because his
return had been a big story in Argentina, and
Rosenfeld was interested, as any psychoanalyst
might have been, not so much in hearing about
Ricardo's murders as about his childhood. Did I
know at what age his mother had left him? he asked
when the concert was over and we were on our way
to dinner. And did I know at what age his father had
died?

When I answered these questions with five and
nine respectively, Rosenfeld said, "Ah. His father

died when he was still little. He may have blamed his mother for 'killing' his father. So when he killed those women, he may have been killing not just the mother he felt had abandoned him, but someone he thought of as a killer herself."

It was fancy footwork, but intriguing, suggesting as it did a reason for Ricardo's always sounding as if his killings were justified, as if the women he'd removed from the world had gotten what they deserved. Interesting, too, was Rosenfeld's fascination when I told him that Ricardo had reported to Dr. Dietz that he always experienced a racing heart and a fluttery feeling in the pit of his stomach just before he murdered. "Panic attacks," Rosenfeld said. "They date from early infancy, you know. The symptoms he describes are what babies experience when they are left alone. Hunger. The feeling of a hole at their center."

By this time we were in the restaurant he had chosen for our post-theater meal, and it was nearly midnight—a not uncommon Argentinian dining hour. I was feeling a bit of a hole at my center, too, I told him, and he ordered us the restaurant's signature squid dish and began questioning me about Ricardo's mother. "What is she like? Is she pretty?"

"I don't know yet," I said between bites. "I haven't met her yet."

"Well, you must find out what she looked like when he was a small boy. You must get to see pictures of her at that time, at the time of his developing sexuality. I can guarantee you that she will have been extremely beautiful, and that she will look like the women he murdered."

At the time, I was too busy gobbling down squid to think much of the remark, but the next day I was to marvel at Rosenfeld's perspicacity.

*   *   *

That next day dawned gray and damp—Buenos Aires, which means "good air," is definitely a misnomer for Argentina's capital, which tends to be unpleasantly humid in both hot weather and cold. I was glad to leave the port city and arrive by plane a couple of hours later at my true destination, Mendoza, where the air was crystalline and the sun was shining on a monumental wall of mountains. The Andes. They were higher than any mountains I had ever seen, and their snow-topped immensity took my breath away.

Alberto was waiting for me in the terminal. He had decided to visit his mother during my own visit and to introduce me personally to her. He'd let me know this back when I was still in New York, and we'd arranged that he would meet me at the airport. So I wasn't surprised to see him. But I was surprised to discover that apparently he intended to introduce me to his mother the minute I arrived. A slim woman in her mid-sixties was standing alongside Alberto.

It was Alicia. "You mustn't stay at a hotel!" she said to me in Spanish as soon as Alberto had introduced us. "I have prepared a room for you in our house." Her deep-set eyes gave her a melancholy look, but she was bobbing her head of curly, gray hair up and down enthusiastically.

"No, no," I demurred, and, speaking English, added, "I don't want to trouble you."

She understood me, just as I'd understood her. We each had a smattering of the other's language. "It would be no trouble," she declared.

I thought, perhaps not. But the last thing in the world I wanted was to spend my time in Mendoza in the bosom of Ricardo Caputo's family. There were things I wanted to do, people I wanted to see whose interchanges with me it might be necessary to keep secret. "Please," I said, "you're very kind. But I think it's best that I stay in a hotel."

She looked disappointed, her eyes growing even sadder and her face, sun-dried and wrinkled, turning away from mine for a moment. But she was determined to be hospitable: "Then come to us for dinner tonight. Everyone's coming. Alberto here, and my second daughter. And her two little girls— my granddaughters. We can get to know each other."

I didn't want to get to know her. Not today. I'd been thinking and thinking about Alicia for weeks, wondering what sort of woman she was, wondering how she coped with having given life to a man as vicious as Ricardo, wondering if I would like or despise her. But I didn't feel ready to find any of this out. I was too tired. The all-night flight to Argentina and my marathon day yesterday had drained me of everything, even of curiosity. I wanted only to withdraw, go to my hotel room and sleep till the next morning.

But Alicia wouldn't hear of it. "Come. We won't talk about anything serious. We won't talk about Cadi." It was her pet name for Ricardo, and I was soon to learn that though he was a grown man and a murderer, she still often called and thought of him as Cadi, her little boy. But at the moment, all I knew about her was that she thought of Alberto as a boy, for she reached out a delicate hand and rumpled his thinning hair. "I have my son back, thanks to you," she said. "He hasn't been home in over a year." And then, still trying to be gracious in the face of my churlishness, she touched me on the arm and implored, "You must come. I've already started preparing the food."

Alberto tried to deflect her. "Linda's tired," he said in Spanish. "She can come to us tomorrow."

"No, no," Alicia rattled in Spanish, "I would feel terrible if we let her spend her first night in Mendoza all alone in a hotel room."

I had understood her, again. And I didn't want her to feel terrible. There was something extraordinarily *simpática* about her, some sweetness that seeped through her sad eyes, weather-beaten skin, and affectionate gestures. And so we negotiated. I would go to my hotel, sleep for a few hours, and then join the family for their nine-o'clock dinner.

I had chosen my hotel, the Plaza, because Alberto had told me that it was in the casino of this very hotel that his and Ricardo's father used to gamble the night away. A turn-of-the-century edifice, its facade and lobby had been lovingly, artistically restored. At the entrance was a colonnade of gilt-trimmed, gleamingly white pillars, a row of handsome brass, antique lampposts, and a colossal cut-glass-and-brass chandelier. But the interior was another matter. The rugs on stairs and corridors were threadbare and torn. The rooms were spartanly furnished, the mattresses saggy, the bathrooms malodorous. I settled into one such room, unheated and drafty in the late-afternoon Andean cold and plagued by a noisy dripping of water from underneath the bathtub. But when Alberto picked me up in the evening and took me to his mother's house, I thanked my lucky stars for having insisted on staying at a hotel, even this one.

It was not because her home wasn't comfortable. A brick house with a crucifix over the door, it wasn't large, but it had an eat-in kitchen, a living room with a gas fireplace and several upholstered couches, and a dining room with enough space for a big table and numerous chairs. But soon after Alicia had shown me around these front rooms and excused herself to do a few last-minute cooking chores, Alberto said with a mischievous smile on his lips, "Come see the bedroom my mother fixed up for you." He led me into a foyer, then opened a locked door. Within was a dark room, and at first I could see nothing. Then Alberto flicked on a light, and I saw a tiny monastic bed in the center of the room and a couple of framed pictures on the walls. Alberto watched my glance settle on one of the pictures, a colorful religious print. *"La Madre de Dios,"* Alberto, still smiling his mischievous smile, said. "My mother hung it specially in your honor."

"Nice of her," I murmured. Alberto stood patiently by, waiting for me to examine the other picture.

That one proved to be a large photograph of a young man standing at the edge of a river dressed in a stylish leather jacket and skintight jeans. His hair was cropped close to his head, like the hair of an ancient Roman emperor, his stance was cocky, hands deep in his back pockets, and his face seemed to be surveying some unseen but pleasing horizon with a determined and confident expression. "Ricardo," Alberto said. "She's kept this picture of him on one wall or another ever since he first left home."

I stared at the picture. And then I shuddered.

Alberto laughed. "I told my mother you wouldn't want to sleep with a picture of Ricardo beaming down at you."

Back in the living room, the other guests had gathered. There was Magda, Alicia's middle daughter, a computer programmer. There was Magda's husband, Luis, and their two young children, Paola and Natalia. And soon, there arrived Luis Pinto, Alicia's husband, home from the flooring factory which had once belonged to Alberto Matias but which Luis and Alicia had managed to buy after they married. He came in apologizing for being late and, sinking his heavy frame down to a child's height, hugged and kissed his granddaughters. I had expected Luis to be brusque, formidable. Ricardo, and even Alberto, had described him as a difficult, punitive parent. But there was no trace of severity in his treatment of his granddaughters. Perhaps he had softened. Or perhaps Ricardo and Alberto, locked into their resentment of him for having stolen away their mother, had provoked in him behaviors that were not natural to him.

Luis produced for me the evidence that Dr. Rosenfeld had suggested I search for—a picture of Alicia during Ricardo's formative years. Luis took it off the mantelpiece to show me how Alicia had looked at the time he first started living with her. I hadn't asked to see such a picture. Not yet. But Luis was an uxorious husband. "This is me," he said, pointing to a slim, energetic-looking youth holding hands with a curvaceous woman. "And this"—his voice filled with pride—"is Alicia."

As Dr. Rosenfeld had predicted, Alicia had indeed resembled the women Ricardo had admitted killing. Her hair, like theirs, was long, her body full, her smile expansive. And like them, each of them, she was beautiful in a natural, artless way.

I saw a remnant of that beauty shortly when I went into the kitchen, to which Alicia's granddaughters had retreated, for in their presence she was animated, exuberant. She was feeding them snacks when I entered, bananas and slices of bread to tide them over until dinner was ready, and soon she began setting them to work at drawing and coloring. She cleared space at the kitchen table, found them paper and crayons, helped them decide what to draw, and when they showed her their creations, profusely admired their little stick people, square houses, and great round suns. Later, when coloring palled, she turned her back on her pots for a while and began making the girls tiny origami vessels from folded scraps of paper, her face wreathed in smiles.

Alicia's mood remained cheerful throughout dinner. I gathered it was rare for her to have a visitor from abroad, and she had certainly fussed over the menu, made a soup, steak, several vegetable casseroles. But at ten-thirty, when Magda and her husband and the two little girls departed for home, Alicia's gaiety faded swiftly. When she rose to clear the table, she moved slowly, and as she began gathering up dishes, her small body seemed to shrink, to fold in upon itself.

"Let me help," I offered.

Alicia nodded, and I followed her into the kitchen with an armload of plates.

Back and forth, back and forth we went, and then Alicia began washing the dishes. By hand, of course. She had no dishwasher, not even, she informed me, a proper clotheswasher, which was what she really wanted. The one she used was barely adequate. Had I seen it?

I hadn't, and she gestured over her shoulder at an alcove where she kept her washing machine. It was a small cylindrical tub, with a separate wringing-out machine that could be attached to it.

"From the year one," I said.

"*Seguro.*"

She was still rinsing dishes, and when I picked up a towel and said I'd help with the drying, she smiled at me gratefully. And then, despite her promise not to discuss Ricardo with me yet, she said, "I do get tired at this hour. And then I always get sad. I think of Cadi. I can't help it. He is the great sadness of my life."

I heard more, much more, about that great sadness the following day when, rested, I sat down in the kitchen with Alicia to do a proper interview with her. She told me the story of her life, her girlhood on the paradisiacal island, her seduction by Alberto Matias, her affair with Luis. I had heard all this from Alberto, of course, but it was different hearing it from Alicia, whose descriptions were ornamented with poetic phrases and minor but telling details. The river that flowed past her island was so busy, she said, that it was "like a street." Alberto Matias, she said, "carried pistols all the time." But the biggest difference between her account of her life and Alberto's account of it was that she was filled with chagrin about how it had worked out. "My biggest sin was to fall in love with Luis," she said when she came to that part of her narrative. "I wasn't a bad woman. And what I did was very common around here. But in our case, destiny gave us a bad hand, and the children were the ones who paid."

"Paid?" I asked. "Paid how?"

"Well, Cadi," she murmured. "He never forgave me. Do you know, a few days after he'd come home and told us all what he'd done, he came to me when I was alone in the kitchen and said to me, 'Mami, why did you leave me? I loved you so much.' And then he grabbed me, and he began shaking me. He shook me so hard that I was afraid he was going to kill *me.* And then he let go and he hit the wall so hard with his fist I thought he was going to break it."

"He has strong hands," I muttered.

"Yes, yes, I know. That's just what *he* said afterward. 'I have strong hands.' "

She was weeping, tears gathering in the lashes of her deep-set eyes. Hoping to deflect her emotionality, I became businesslike, professional. "I'd like to ask you more about those first few days after he came home. Did he say he wanted to turn himself in? Did he say why?"

My technique worked. She pulled herself together and began to talk about Ricardo's return to Mendoza. It was a tale rich with maternal denial. "We hadn't heard from Cadi in more than twenty years. I thought he was dead or else living in some jungle somewhere. I didn't know about his killings—well, just about the first one. But he'd been engaged to that first girl, and I'd always figured that she must have been unfaithful and that's why he killed her. That's a terrible thing to do, but it's not uncommon around here. But the other killings? No, I knew nothing about them. Sure, the police came here looking for him many times. But they didn't say why they were looking for him. And sure, people told me there'd been articles in the papers saying that he'd killed again, but I didn't think the articles could be true. What I thought was, just because he did that first killing, they're accusing him of others.

"Then, last year, Luis and I were sitting here in the house and the phone rang, and when Luis picked it up, a man who wouldn't give his name asked to speak to me. Luis put me on, but the man still wouldn't give his name. He just said, 'You know me, but you haven't spoken to me in a long time.' I was annoyed, because we sometimes get nuisance calls, and so I handed the phone back to Luis, and he said, 'Don't bother us or I'm going to trace this call and they're going to find you.' And then the man said, 'Please don't hang up. Please let me speak to Señora Alicia again,' and Luis put his hand over the receiver and said in a strange voice, 'You'd better talk to this guy.' Some sixth sense had told him it was Ricardo. And it was. He was phoning, he said, from Buenos Aires. And he was taking a bus to Mendoza and we should pick him up the next day at the bus terminal."

As Alicia was telling me this, Luis, who had been talking to Alberto in the living room, wandered into the kitchen and sat down alongside us. "He started with a lie to begin with," Luis interrupted the account. "Later we learned that he was already in Mendoza when he called. But when he first called, he pretended he wasn't—why I could never understand."

Alicia frowned at Luis and went on with her tale. "He told us how he would be dressed, in case we couldn't recognize him, and the next day we went to the bus station."

"I was the one who went inside," Luis said. "Even just what I'd heard so far worried me, so I took precautions. I made Alicia stay in the car, and I went into the station. I had no trouble recognizing him. He was the same, only heavier and with less hair."

"He got into the back of the car with me," Alicia continued, "and his first words to me were, 'Mama, Mama, I thought you had died!' And then he said he'd done a lot of bad things. But he didn't say what. Just that his life was a misery, and he was sorry for all the bad things he'd done. We didn't know what those things were until the next day, when he told us he'd killed four women."

"No, we didn't know there were four killings until later, after he saw the lawyer," Luis dissented. "When he started talking, at first he said he'd only committed two murders. Then he said there'd been a third one, too."

"I went cold when he talked to us about the murders," Alicia broke in. "But I'm very strong. I listened to everything. I didn't get hysterical. I contained myself, in order to give him strength."

"Strength for what?" I asked.

"To turn himself in," she replied.

"Was it his idea?"

"Oh, yes," Alicia said. "From the very beginning, he wanted to turn himself in."

This time, she and Luis were in agreement. "Yes, yes," Luis affirmed, "he wanted to turn himself in."

I wasn't sure I believed them. Alberto had mentioned that Ricardo had hoped his family might find some way to hide him. But they said nothing about this and, remaining steadfastly loyal to their black sheep, insisted that surrender had been in his mind from the start. Still, from something Alicia said next, I gathered that other alternatives were considered, or at least discussed. "I wasn't sure if surrendering himself was such a good idea," she said. "But then I thought, what if he kills again? And I went against my heart and told him to give himself up. It was a terrible decision for a mother to make."

"I'm sure it was."

"It gives me a knot in my heart," Alicia sighed. "But I felt that if he came forward, he could feel free within himself. And that if he felt free within himself, even if he was locked up, he would be as free as we are."

Even if he was locked up, he would be as free as we are. The sentiment was similar to the one that Kennedy at his first press conference had attributed to Ricardo: "He told me," the lawyer had said, 'I would rather have my body locked up and my mind free than my mind locked up and my body free.' It was a very spiritual concept, and I now felt certain it had originated with the devout Alicia. I also felt certain that, just as Alberto had suggested, it was

Alicia who had sparked in Ricardo the notion that
assuming a penitent stance and pleading remorse
might bring him some benefit, for she was going on,
"After he confessed to all that he'd done, he said,
'Mami, help me to turn myself in.' I held his hand
and told him that it's very easy for a person who's
done nothing wrong to be good. The hard thing is to
admit that you've done wrong and say, 'I won't do it
again.' And I talked to him about God.

"It seemed to calm him. He said, 'Teach me how
to pray again.' I gave him a Bible and we started
praying. And I told him, 'I admire your valor in
coming here and telling the truth. And I know that
if you are truly sorry for what you have done, God
will forgive you.'

"'And you, Mama?' he said. 'Are you going to forgive me?'"

"I said, 'If you are truly sorry for what you did, I
forgive you.' And I hugged him."

Ricardo, both Alicia and Luis agreed, had been
very alarming in the first days he was home. He had
alternated between loquaciousness and sullenness,
had paced up and down like a caged animal, and
had sometimes smiled but more often grimaced, a
hard expression forming in his eyes. Luis had been
frightened of him, not so much for himself, but for
Alicia, and for their youngest daughter, Susana,
who was living at home while doing a medical resi-
dency at the local hospital. Luis put locks on the
bedroom doors. He asked Magda and her children,
as well as Alicita, the daughter he and Alicia had
had before they married and who lived now on a
farm in the countryside, to visit the house as often
as they could. And he loaded his hunting rifle and
slept with it beneath his pillow.

But if he was afraid that Ricardo might harm his

mother or Susana, Luis was also frightened by the mere fact of allowing his long-hunted stepson to stay in the family home. If Interpol discovered his presence, Luis feared, he and Alicia could be accused of harboring a criminal. As soon as Ricardo said he was certain he wanted to turn himself in, Luis took him to see a lawyer, his friend Mario Luquez, in the hopes that once he did so, the lawyer and not the family would be responsible for Ricardo.

They visited Luquez one January afternoon. The lawyer made Luis sit in his waiting room while he talked to Ricardo alone, then he called Luis in and said that Ricardo had confessed to certain crimes that had been committed in Mexico and the United States, was prepared to turn himself in for them, but hoped that if he did, he would then be sent to a psychiatric hospital.

To accomplish this, the lawyer said, it would be necessary for Ricardo to start seeing a psychiatrist. He made a recommendation, a man with whom he had worked in the past. And he warned Luis that he should drive Ricardo to and from his visits to the psychiatrist and see to it that he didn't go off anywhere on his own, for if he did, he might be recognized and arrested before the lawyer could negotiate his surrender. If that happened, the family could be charged with harboring a criminal.

The next few weeks were hellish. Ricardo had to make regular visits to both the lawyer and the psychiatrist, but frequently he objected to being escorted. Luis, who had taken to hiding Ricardo in the back of his truck when he drove him to his appointments, tried to reason with him, and sometimes it worked, but sometimes Ricardo rebelled, insisted on walking home and doing so all by himself; Luis would nervously trail him at a distance. Ricardo also seemed incapable of getting it through his head that he was not to talk to anyone. One day he demanded that Luis take him to a bookstore, and at the store he got into a chatty conversation with another shopper. After a few minutes the man said to Ricardo that he thought they'd met once before at a disco, but he couldn't remember his name. Luis, who had been standing a few feet away and listening to the conversation, hurried over and whisked Ricardo out of the store.

But this close call was nothing compared to other problems that Ricardo continually created for the family. He refused to follow the proscription the psychiatrist, who had begun giving him anti-agitation medication, had insisted on: no alcohol. At meals, he would demand wine, and only Susana, who was herself a doctor, was able to argue him out of his craving. And worse, one day Ricardo demanded that Luis find him a woman. Luis went into a panic and called the psychiatrist, who gave Ricardo an injection that would control his sexual appetite.

Luis felt so stressed by Ricardo's presence that he wasn't surprised when, several weeks after his errant stepson had returned home, he felt pains in his chest. "I got involved too much," he said. "And I was trying to do everything myself. I had a heart attack."

He was hospitalized for five days, and those days were horrifying to him, not just because he had nearly died, but because he was away from home, no longer able to supervise Ricardo. But nothing untoward happened in his absence, and soon after he returned home, weak but on the mend, the lawyer concluded the arrangements for Ricardo's surrender in the United States. At once, Alberto was summoned from the United States to deliver

Ricardo into the hands of Michael Kennedy, and right after his arrival, he departed with Ricardo in tow and the family's ordeal was over. "I feel good now," Luis said, explaining all he'd been through. "Good in my health. And good about Ricardo, too. Because I think I did the right thing. If I had let him go free and he had killed someone else, it would have been on my conscience."

We broke for lunch soon after I heard the story of Luis's heart attack. Alberto had gone out, but he returned and we sat down to another elaborate meal. During it, Alicia talked wistfully about the future. "I still want in the years left to me to do a lot of things. I would like to see Ricardo's kids. I would like to have an automatic washing machine. And I would like to have my poems published."

"Your poems?" I said. "I didn't know you wrote poetry."

"Oh, I do. I even took a writing course and got a diploma. I'll show it to you."

"I'd rather see your poems. I'd love to see your poems."

Alicia rose, went into her bedroom, and returned with several small notebooks filled with handwritten stanzas. Seeing them, I thought of the poetry Ricardo had years ago written for Judith Becker. Poems of seduction. But Alicia's poems were different, were filled, just as she was, with an overarching melancholy.

The first poem I looked at was called "Pampeana," which Alicia translated for me as "a zamba, a dance from the pampas." *Traigo esta zamba lejana*, it began, *zamba que viene del sur, en las llanuras pampeanas, zambita querida, de me juventud.* In English, it reads:

* * *

I bring this distant *zamba*,
a *zamba* that comes from the south
in the plains of the pampas,
the dear little *zamba*
of my youth.
The guitars lulled me,
the ombu tree saw my birth
the lark sang to me,
and I grew like the ostrich
running over those fields.
Thus was my youth.

When I have sorrows,
I feel like singing
and making flowers out of my grief
in order not to cry.
I feel like singing to the wind
of the pampas
asking it to take my pain away.

And when on clear nights
I see the Southern Cross shine,
I remember my mother singing
the dear little *zamba*
of my youth.
And I want to sing
that little *zamba* of yesteryear,
that *zamba* I brought from the south.

Many of the other poems were about Ricardo
and had been written during the years Alicia had
longed to see him again. There was "Hijo," son:

Yes, you were part of my body.
In my own soul,
Your small being.
I brought you into the world

And I loved your presence.
How can I resign myself
To not seeing you again.

And there was "Ricardito Amado," beloved little Ricardo:

In this night full of stars
my thoughts fly
and take me to your side
where I look at how beautiful you are.

How very distant was that afternoon
when you left without returning.
Dear son, I always wait for you.
My eyes long to see you arrive.

Poor Alicia, I thought as I read this poem. Her long wait had ended, her eyes had seen her son arrive, but that arrival had hardly made her happy. Nothing did. Could. Not even the considerable accomplishments of her other children. Alberto was a rich and successful businessman. Alicita owned a farm. Magda was a computer expert. Susana was a medical doctor. No matter. Ricardo was a murderer, and Alicia, who had lived so long with denial, would never get over that now at long last irrefutable fact.

That afternoon, Alberto, no doubt feeling as touched by his mother's predicament as I was, impulsively decided to make one of her wishes come true. He drove, with me, to an appliance store on one of Mendoza's main streets. The shop was crammed with washing machines, many of them as antique-looking as the small cylindrical one with separate wringer that Alicia already owned. But a few resembled the standard American washing machine, sleek, waist-high, rectangular affairs that featured a damp-dry spin cycle. Alberto wanted one of these.

We examined them, assessing their dimensions and capacity, and with my advice Alberto finally settled on one of the smaller machines, for it had seemed to me that Alicia's kitchen could hardly accommodate a larger one. Even so, the price was astronomical. "That's one thousand one hundred twenty-four U.S. dollars," the clerk told us. "But if you pay cash, you can have it for one thousand dollars."

Alberto didn't hesitate. "I'll take it," he said, peeling greenbacks from his wallet. "But on one condition. I want it delivered this afternoon." To me, he explained, "I want to see my mother's face when it comes, and who knows what time we'll be over at the house tomorrow."

This was true. I had called the two psychiatrists who had treated Ricardo, Dr. Ernesto Padin who had seen him when he was an adolescent, and Dr. Fernando Linares, who had seen him after he returned home last year. Linares had refused to meet with me but Padin had said he would call me tomorrow and give me an appointment sometime that day. When I'd told Alberto this, he'd begged to accompany me, and I had said he could, provided Padin had no objection.

"So?" Alberto was saying now to the appliance clerk, who was staring as if mesmerized at the greenbacks. "Is it a deal?"

"I think so," the stunned clerk said. "I guess so." A moment later, he called over the manager, and the manager promised immediate delivery.

Alberto wasn't disappointed in the reaction his impetuous generosity produced. We went back to the house, and when the delivery men arrived, Alicia watched with confusion as they unwrapped their huge parcel. Then she said, "What is it?"

"*Una máquina,*" one of the men said. A washing machine.

"No." Alicia shook her head and, as if when she had dreamed of owning a new washing machine, she had imagined one that would look just like the one she already had, insisted, "That's not a washing machine. What is it?"

"It *is* a washing machine, *Mamita,*" Alberto gloated. "From me and Kim. Look. Look how it works." He opened the lid, and Alicia peered suspiciously inside.

"It's huge," she said when she raised her head. "I don't have enough laundry for it. I'll have to do Magda's, too." And then Alicia gave one of her rare smiles, a mischievous smile, just like the one that sometimes lit up Alberto's face. "And the neighbors'. I'll have to do the neighbors' laundry, too."

Alberto and I went out to dinner that night at the home of a childhood friend of his, a prosperous man named Guillermo Villanueva, who owned both a busy cement factory and a fashionable ski resort. Guillermo and his wife, Beatriz, lived in an elegant section of Mendoza in a penthouse apartment overlooking a vast park. They sat us down on overstuffed couches, poured us several glasses of the excellent local champagne, and finally, at ten o'clock, directed us to the dining room for dinner— steak, of course, but this time, filet mignon.

Guillermo was aware that I was in Mendoza to do research about Ricardo. "It's a puzzling case," he said as he opened a numbered bottle of a ruby-colored Mendoza wine. "I knew Ricardo as a boy, and I cannot understand how he came to do the things he did."

"Did you know him well?" I asked.

"No. I was Alberto's friend. Ricardo was younger. A bit of a liar, but otherwise a nice enough kid. Quiet."

"So much for outward appearances," Beatriz commented. Then she said that like everyone else in Mendoza, she and Guillermo had followed every detail of Ricardo's case, but that they had done so because they had a special interest in the case.

"Because Guillermo knew Ricardo as a child?" I asked.

"No," Beatriz said. "Because Guillermo—"

"Because my sister," Guillermo interrupted, "my sister Graciela, who will be joining us shortly for dessert, is best friends with the wife of Dr. Linares, the psychiatrist who treated Ricardo last year."

I'd had a lot of champagne and wine by then, but I became alert in a second. "Is Graciela close with Dr. Linares, too?"

"Yes, certainly."

"I'd been hoping to see Linares. But he wouldn't agree to an interview."

"Oh"—Guillermo waved a hand in the air— "Graciela will get him to see you."

Not long afterward, Graciela arrived. A teacher of literature in a local college, she was interested in talking to me about writing and writers, and for a while we discussed Bellow and Updike, Borges and Cortázar. But after a time I let literature fall by the wayside and poured out to her my disappointment about coming all this way and not being able to see Linares. "I'll speak to him," Graciela promised. "No problem."

Guillermo nodded approvingly. He was one of those hosts who not only want to wine and dine his guests royally, but see to all their needs.

Perhaps that was why, at around one in the morning when we finally launched in upon our dessert, Guillermo offered me a rare piece of information, one that I suppose Beatriz had almost revealed to me earlier. "You know," he said, "I saw Ricardo here in Mendoza back in 1974 or 1975."

"But he couldn't have been here," I at first discounted Guillermo's claim. "The police were hunting for him. He'd never have come back here."

"I saw him, I tell you," Guillermo insisted. "I ran into him on the Avenida San Martin, and he told me he'd killed another woman. Not the one we all knew about, the one he'd been engaged to."

I was astonished. "He just came out with such damning information?"

"Yes, that he'd killed another woman. In the United States."

I found this exceedingly interesting for it reminded me of something Gorden McEwan had said, namely that his informant had reported that in a moment of braggadocio Ricardo had volunteered to him, too, that he'd killed a woman—in his case, Jacqui Bernard. Remembering, I shook my head and told the Villanuevas the story, remarking when I was done, "You'd think he'd keep things like that to himself. But apparently, he was proud of his killings."

"Yes and no," Guillermo said. "He may have been boasting, but his tone wasn't boastful. It was matter-of-fact. What he said to me, he said in such an ordinary tone of voice that I didn't believe him. I thought it was one of his lies."

"Did he say anything more?"

"No. Just that he was glad to be back. I took him to a café and bought him a cup of coffee."

"Everyone was looking for him," Alberto exclaimed. "The FBI, Interpol. And he went out with you for coffee?"

"Yes. I suppose, in retrospect, that he felt invisible."

"Innocent," Graciela, the literature teacher, said. "In the way Raskolnikov felt innocent. As if he had more of a right to life than the women he killed had."

15

The very next day, I met with Dr. Linares. Graciela had kept her word and asked him to see me, and he had agreed, but requested that I bring both Graciela and Alberto along. "Why?" I'd asked Graciela. "Because," she'd explained, "apparently, he had some difficulties with Ricardo's family. They accused him of saying things to the press here that he never said. So he wants witnesses to his conversation with you."

He needn't have made such a stipulation. He said nothing damaging to Ricardo, nothing that, as far as I could tell, violated patient-doctor confidentiality. Indeed, he was as restrained—and as theoretical—as a psychiatric textbook. "You understand," he said when he shook my hand in greeting, "I will reveal no secrets. I will talk about patients *like* Ricardo. That is all I will do."

That was out in the waiting room, a tiny alcove with so few seats that Graciela had to perch on an end table. Inside his office, a dimly lit room dominated by a blackboard and an elevated desk, he announced, "I know it is customary to term someone like Ricardo a sociopath or psychopath. But according to German psychiatry, which I find far more devoted to fine discriminations of symptoms than your American psychiatry, an interesting percentage of psychopathic personalities are brain-damaged. I believe this may be the case with Ricardo." And at this, Linares, a chunky man with salt-and-pepper hair and a little mustache and beard, seated himself behind the thronelike desk, motioned the rest of us to take places on a low Naugahyde couch, and began to lecture us about one of the latest developments in the field of psychiatry—the search for the physiological cause of psychopathy.

"What makes a psychopath?" he said. "Why should someone grow up without a conscience? Without sympathy? It cannot just be rearing. It must be a brain abnormality. There is research that is beginning to show this. There are brilliant doctors who even as we speak are finding the sources of violent behavior in brain lesions, temporal-lobe epilepsy, ictal phenomena in the limbic system."

Alberto and Graciela looked stunned and uncomprehending, perhaps because Linares was talking in English, but more likely, since both of them knew English quite well, because he was being so technical. I, however, understood perfectly what Linares was talking about. My husband, who had for years done research in neuropsychology, had often told me about the search for the neurological cause of violence. But what my husband had said was that the search was still in its squalling infancy and not likely for decades to influence the legal determination of sanity. Linares had a different view, a belief in an imminent and happy future that would any day now explain the biological nature of criminality and allow felons to plead not guilty by virtue of their unfortunate biology. "Ricardo is a sick man," he said, waxing exuberant. "Can anyone who knows what he did deny this? No! Therefore, his lawyers in America must get psychiatrists who will look for his

brain damage. Then, when they find it, and I am
certain it will be found, he will not need to be in a
prison but can go to a mental hospital."

It was hard to get a word in edgewise, but I tried:
"I don't know that even if a neuropsychiatrist found
some brain abnormality, it would count for much in
a court of law. Not in the United States. Have you
had repeat murderers here in Argentina who have
been able to win an insanity defense on the basis of
an irregular CAT scan?"

"I don't know," Linares huffed. "I am not a forensic psychiatrist. I attend neurotic and depressed
patients primarily. But I have done a lot of reading
in this area, and I believe that Ricardo must have a
neurological lesion."

All this time I had been wondering what the
blackboard was for, but now I found out, for he
stood up, drew two large overlapping chalk circles
on the board, and labeled one of them "neurological
disease" and the other "psychopathic personality."
Then he raised his chalk, looked meaningfully at the
three of us, and drew a thick line through the circles
to separate them. "In time to come, we will not
lump these two together," he said exhaling. "In time
to come, they will be separate phenomena."

Linares was so passionate about his notions that
for a moment—was it possible?—I found myself feeling sorry for Ricardo. He must have sat here in this
office, I thought, listened to the enthusiastic Dr.
Linares, and himself come to believe that if he turned
himself in, he would as a matter of course be sent not
to a prison but to a psychiatric hospital. That would
have pleased him, for he knew the ropes in American
psychiatric hospitals, had once managed to escape
from one. But if Ricardo had cynically wanted to be
in a hospital, Linares's reasons for wanting to see him
in one were not cynical. He viewed a medical setting

as the proper place for Ricardo because he sincerely believed that extreme behavior like Ricardo's was a medical problem, physiological in origin and therefore potentially responsive to some as yet unknown treatment and cure.

Such beliefs are idealistic, but they are vastly comforting to criminals and their families. Indeed, for a moment, even the pragmatic Alberto seemed inclined to sign on for the hunt for the elusive physical origin of violence. "Could violence be caused by tuberculosis?" he suddenly asked. "When he was little, Ricardo had tuberculosis."

"It's possible," Linares said. "I don't recall reading anything about tuberculosis and violence, but it's possible that there have been studies. I could look the matter up for you, but it would be a lot of work, take me a great deal of time."

At the mention of work, Alberto's interest subsided. "No, no, I was just wondering."

Linares looked disappointed. He was a true scholar, one who would have relished collecting research, however irrelevant to Ricardo's future it might have been.

The air had turned chilly and a stiff wind was blowing when Graciela, Alberto, and I left Linares's office. "The *zonda*," Graciela said. "We'd better make tracks." Like most Mendozans, she was afraid of the desert windstorm that frequently visited the city, sweeping paper and leaves through the streets, ripping the branches from trees, and depositing clouds of stinging dust that were said to be laden with disease. But the storm was just gathering force. Graciela took a moment to ask whether I could come to dinner at her house on the weekend, and only after I said, yes, I'd love to, hugged me and darted into her car.

I got into Alberto's. My next appointment was with Dr. Ernesto Padin, the doctor who had been on the staff of the psychiatric hospital to which Ricardo had—famously—committed himself when he was but an adolescent, and I had obtained Padin's permission to bring Alberto along.

Padin's waiting room was, if anything, smaller than Linares's. But it was jammed, so packed with people that although it had lots of chairs, there weren't enough to go around, and Alberto had to stand up until one became vacant. Argentina has a plethora of psychiatrists and psychiatric patients. Indeed, as the distinguished Latin American journalist Alma Guillermoprieto has observed, visiting a psychoanalyst four times a week is one of the country's most cherished rituals. Still, no matter how many psychiatrists Argentina has, there aren't enough to go around—or at least, that was the feeling I had sitting in Padin's crowded antechamber. But at last a receptionist, apologizing vociferously for the delay, beckoned us into the consulting room.

It was a tiny, cell-like space with a small desk, a few small chairs, and no couch—Padin was not a psychoanalyst but an eclectic practitioner of his profession. A tall man with sparkling obsidian eyes, he greeted us warmly and said to Alberto, "I believe you were in the military when I knew your brother."

"I was. And I never got straight just exactly what happened to Ricardo at the hospital. Which was why I wanted to come along with Linda."

"No problem," Padin said. "I can understand your interest."

"Do you remember Ricardo?" I asked when we were all seated.

"I never forgot him. His case was most unusual."

"Is he a schizophrenic?" Alberto interrupted,

though I had warned him to let me ask the questions. "He says that when he was at the hospital here, you diagnosed him as a schizophrenic."

The doctor laughed. "Yes, he would say that." Then he leaned forward on his desk, his dark eyes flashing, and said, "Your brother did not have a psychosis. He had *psicopatía*. One of his characteristics was that he always told lies, made up complicated stories. And these stories had one thing in common—they were designed to bring him some kind of benefit. So I am sure that if he has said he was schizophrenic, he imagined that that, too, would bring him a benefit."

Which of course was true. Ricardo had hoped, at the time he turned himself in and claimed a history of schizophrenia, to be confined in a mental hospital. I started to say this to Padin, but he was going on, "As a matter of fact, when I heard that Ricardo had killed lots of people, I at first doubted that it could be true. I believed he might be saying even this in order to obtain some sort of benefit."

"What kind of benefit could come out of saying one had killed several people?" I asked, puzzled.

"Fame. Attention. Money. I am not saying these *were* Ricardo's motives. Just that given how he used to behave, it was a thought that crossed my mind."

Padin then told us how Ricardo used to behave. And what he told us was so reminiscent of the behavior of the adult Ricardo that Alberto and I kept nodding our heads to his words. "Ricardo came to El Sause, the Mendoza psychiatric hospital, when he was around seventeen or eighteen. I was a young man then, a recent graduate of medical school. But I can give you Ricardo's diagnosis with calm and confidence because it was not mine alone. The case was so special that those of us who examined Ricardo filmed our interviews with him and presented his case before the entire hospital staff. It was studied and discussed by professors at the university, and the diagnosis was confirmed by them. Psychopathy.

"We had suspected this from the first. When he came to the hospital, Ricardo told us he was depressed. But he did not seem depressed. His mood appeared to be normal, and he was pleasant and charming and interested in having everyone be fond of him, which is not often the case with depressed patients. He was also very manipulative. He told us he had no place to stay, so we treated him as an inpatient. But he knew someone who worked at the hospital, and I think he thought of it as a good place to live. Certainly, the whole time he was with us, he wanted whatever was the best that the hospital could offer—the best place to sleep, the best food. And to get these things, he would manipulate anybody and anything he could.

"He had been living on the streets until he came to us. And he told us some things about how he made his living. He sold himself sexually to wealthy homosexuals in order to obtain money and expensive clothes. But he himself liked girls, he said, and he also obtained money from them on occasion. One thing that was notable about him was that he had absolutely no scruples. He would seduce the girls by telling them lies about his family."

"What sort of lies?" I asked.

"Oh, that his father had been a rich Italian count."

The mention of his father made Alberto suddenly leap again into the role of questioner. "But of what importance are such lies? I, too, told lies about my father. I remember once telling a girl whose father was a lawyer that mine was a lawyer, too. And both Ricardo and I told lies about our stepfather. When he first came to live with us, we were ashamed, and we said he was a cousin of our mother's."

The doctor shrugged. "Ricardo's lies were constant."

"Yes," Alberto subsided. He had had plenty of experience of them.

"And how *is* your mother?" Padin inquired.

"She's not doing so well," Alberto, who was increasingly taking over the interview, said. "And I worry about her. She feels guilty about Ricardo and mulls over everything that ever happened when he was little, finding fault with herself as a mother."

The doctor nodded. "I imagine Ricardo would not be unhappy to hear that. When he was at the hospital, he always complained about your mother, about how she left the two of you alone with your father, and about how when she came back, she always deferred to your stepfather. But basically, what he was doing was blaming his family for what he was. He took no responsibility for himself. He had absolutely no ethics. Well, there you have it—your classic antisocial personality disorder."

"Full-blown, when he was an adolescent?"

"It generally is."

"But what about adulthood? Could you have predicted the course his antisocial personality disorder would take?"

"Not precisely. Still, we know that adolescent males with this disorder often turn out to be dangerous criminals of one sort or another."

"But what is the cause of the disorder?" Alberto again interrupted. And after mentioning, as he had to Linares, Ricardo's bout with tuberculosis, but this time receiving no support for that theory, he said worriedly, "Can it be the environment in which he grew up? I myself have some similarities to my brother, so perhaps it is the environment. Our childhoods. Our home life."

Dr. Padin must have recognized a subtext in what

Alberto was saying, understood that he was anxious about sharing some characteristics with his brother, for Padin said, "We do not know what causes this personality disorder, but I do not think you need to worry about resembling Ricardo. You are obviously very different. You are, for one thing, concerned about your mother. He had an innate selfishness. He was concerned about no one."

Alberto looked relieved. And in that moment I understood what I had only vaguely comprehended before, namely that one of the reasons he had lent himself to my endeavor was that he had been hoping to obtain precisely the reassurance he had just now received.

Outside on the street, where the wind was beginning to blow ever more strongly, Alberto thanked me cheerfully for having let him come on the interview. I was glad that he felt happy, but I myself was feeling sad. Hearing Padin describe how Ricardo had already been seducing women with his lies when he was not much more than a boy had made me think of Natalie and Judith, Barbara and Laura, and remember how easily he had charmed them. And how brutally he had killed them. Natalie, her flesh perforated a dozen times over with her mother's fish-boning knife. Judith, her nose and cheekbones shattered and her nylon stocking twisted around her throat. Barbara, her face barely recognizable and her skull cracked by the repeated thrust of a stomping boot. Laura, her forehead and jaw smashed to a bloody pulp by a steel bar. Ricardo, I thought, had been in training for his encounters with his victims long before he ever met them, and although his potential dangerousness had been recognized, no one had stepped in to control or limit it.

This had not been the fault of Padin and his fellow doctors. Our society, whether north or south of the border, does not allow the insights of psychiatrists to serve it in any preventive way. I knew this, understood all the reasons, some of them good, why it was so. And yet I found myself thinking unhappily about how vulnerable women are and hopelessly wishing that Padin and his colleagues had been able to file their report on Ricardo in some great registry to which women, all women, could have had access.

My mood didn't lift throughout the entire evening, despite—or perhaps because of—the fact that Alberto and I went out to dinner with Guillermo to eat the traditional *parillada*, steer and cow innards that included kidneys, sweetbreads, even udders. And it seemed to me fitting that when we left the restaurant, the *zonda* was at last in full force, a swirling, biting wind that stung the flesh and gouged at nostrils and eyes. I had changed hotels by then, was staying at a more comfortable and modern establishment than I had at first, and my wall of glass windows rattled and shook and sounded as if it might shatter at any moment. I lay on my bed, unable to sleep, both from the racket the wind was making and from the images that the meeting with Padin had called back into my mind.

Writing about murderers is a manageable occupation provided one merely keeps one's attention on matters at hand, on the interviews that must be arranged, the questions that must be asked. Remembering the murderers' crimes upsets that it's-just-a-job applecart, and produces not just sleeplessness but the sense that the job cannot be done, that none of one's words will ever adequately reflect the images that, once readmitted to memory, tyrannize the brain.

16

I was lethargic and out of sorts the next few days. But Mendoza began to work a certain magic on me. It was a lovely city, one of the oldest in Argentina, and although earthquakes had destroyed most of its colonial architecture, the town had numerous parks, long, tree-lined avenues, and of course, the spectacular backdrop of the Andes. I went up into the mountains one day with Alicia and Luis and Alberto. We had lunch at a little inn that provided a clear view of Aconcagua, the highest mountain in the Western Hemisphere, and after lunch we walked along stony rills replete with sweet-smelling desert flowers and intricate thorny bushes. Alicia was interested in collecting the leaves of a particular plant that were said to cure rheumatism, and she and Luis, arm in arm, moved slowly, eyes to the earth, supporting one another on the treacherous ground. Looking down on their slow progress from a height well beyond them, I found it difficult to imagine this elderly, devoted couple as responsible in any way for what the wretched Ricardo had become.

It was even more difficult on a subsequent afternoon, when the family gathered for a festive weekend lunch. Alicia was going to make *empanadas,* her spe-

cialty, and she had started the preparations early in
the morning, stirring the traditional chipped beef
and raisins in one huge pot and in another a brew of
cornmeal and white sauce for Luis, who since his
heart attack was trying to limit his beef intake. When
I arrived at the house, there was still work to be done.
The fillings Alicia had cooked had to be sealed into
little doughy pockets, which could then be brushed
with egg, baked in the oven, and put under a broiler
to gain the classic golden brown *empanada* color.
Alberto had been drafted to do the sealing and was
tracing a watery finger along the edges of circlets of
dough, then laboriously crimping and indenting
them. Luis, too, was helping, running the oven and
broiler. The kitchen was hot, floury, redolent, and
Alicia was commanding her troops like a gentle general. I pitched in, too, and by the time Magda and her
husband and the two little granddaughters arrived,
we had made scores of tiny pies, nearly all of which
were consumed during a three-hour lunch.

The dinner to which Graciela had invited me was
that same evening. Like Alicia's lunch, it was a family affair, a meeting of a cousins' club that ren-
dezvoused once a month or so. Graciela had com-
mandeered her building's *asado*, a room in the base-
ment designed for barbecue parties, and her brother Guillermo and several of his male cousins were
tending thick slabs of steak over a sizzling fire. A
few outsiders, such as myself, had been invited,
among them Dr. Linares and a guitar player famous
for his tangos, and when the beef was deemed
ready, we all sat down at a long, narrow table and
dined on it and on salads of tomatoes and pota-
toes—that is, the women did. The men, I noticed,
consumed nothing but the meat.

At one-thirty in the morning, when the meal was

finished, I thought the evening was over. But in fact, it was just beginning. We left the *asado*, took the elevator up to Graciela's penthouse, and settled down in comfort to drink champagne, eat strawberry shortcake, and hear the tango player.

I was lulled by the heavy food and copious wine and for a brief while forgot that I had come to Mendoza on a mission, that I had been hoping that somehow here I might discover the source of the *Clarín* article Elise McCarthy had so long ago shown me and with it the true reason Ricardo had turned himself in. Nothing except getting to know my newfound companions and listening to the haunting sounds of the tango singer seemed to matter. *"Volver, con la frente marchita,"* the singer was intoning as he strummed his guitar, *"las nieves del tiempo platearon mi sien."* It was a song about a man returning home after a long absence, the snows of time having withered his brow and silvered his temples.

"Do you dance the tango at home?" Guillermo asked me when the song was done.

"Yes, I adore it. It's so sensual and sinuous."

"But it is not really a dance, is it?" Linares said. "It is more, as we say here, a sad feeling to which one moves."

This was interesting to me, for like most Americans, I thought of the tango as a dance of seduction not sorrow. I mentioned this to Linares and he said, "Yes and no. It started as a dance that men who had come to this country from distant places and were far from their wives and families performed alone. Then the local prostitutes began doing it with them, doing it in order to seduce them. The prostitutes were sexy, inviting. But the men were never altogether free of guilt or nostalgia or sorrow when they danced with these women. You have only to listen to the words of tango songs to

understand this. Have you noticed that the words
are invariably about lost love, lost friendship, lost
opportunity? Tango songs are lamentations—the
music of the human psyche, as it were."

"Do the Mendoza song for Linda," Graciela
directed the singer.

"Yes, the Mendoza song," Guillermo echoed her.

The guitar player began to strum, a lilting,
lamenting sound, and then his voice lifted in an ode
to the city. Mendoza, he sang, was more beautiful
than any other place on earth, especially in the
autumn, when the leaves turn to orange and red.
Mendoza, he sang, was a place where one could feel
true friendship.

I was back on track the next afternoon. On my
behalf, Luis had called Mario Luquez, the lawyer
who had arranged Ricardo's surrender to Michael
Kennedy, and Luquez had scheduled an appointment with Alberto and me.

When we arrived, he wasn't in his office—"delayed
in court," his secretary advised me. We sat down to
wait for him in a dimly lit anteroom where the seats
were backless stools and there was nothing to read
but shabby magazines that were two and three years
old. I imagined the lawyer would prove to be similarly shabby, but after an hour or so, a tall man with
shiny black hair slicked back in the style once affected by Juan Perón and wearing a stylish formal coat
entered the anteroom and hurried grandly past us,
looking neither to the left or right but leaving in his
wake a heavy scent of pomade. It was Luquez, and
we were soon called upstairs to his office, where, the
coat removed to display an immaculate white shirt
and expensive-looking gray tweed jacket, he rose
imposingly from behind a large desk.

His costume was elegant but his face was even

more so. Thin and long, with sunken cheeks and an
upper lip that was a mere tight stripe, it was the face
of an aging toreador.

"You have come about Ricardo Caputo?" he said,
and shook my hand. His fingers, the nails elabo-
rately manicured, were also thin and long. "I know
no English, señora," he said as they grasped mine,
his Spanish as formal and exquisite as his attire.
"And I cannot tell you much. I am bound by a professional code."

I sat down, placed my tape recorder on his vast
desk, and said, "I understand. Just say whatever you
feel comfortable about saying."

"And you are going to tape me?"

"Yes."

"Is that necessary?" He pointed a long finger at
the little machine as if he were leveling a picador's
lance at some doomed animal.

We are in the bullring, for sure, I thought; there's
no way I'm going to interview this man without getting his responses on the record. I said, "Yes. I don't
write Spanish very well, and it would be exceedingly difficult for me to take notes in that language and
keep an interview going."

Luquez saw the sense to that, and when I turned
on the machine, he began talking to it without further ado.

"Ricardo came to my office on January twenty-
first, 1994. He was brought by Mr. Luis Pinto, for
whom I once handled a civil matter. That summer
afternoon was very warm. Ricardo started telling
me all that had happened to him. We talked for a
few hours. I was astonished. I turned pale listening
to what he had to relate. And I thought he was making it up. He related things that had happened from
the 1970s to the present day, a story of twenty-four
years, with all the details, the names, cities, person-

alities, everything. And he asked me to make the necessary arrangements to get him into a psychiatric hospital.

"I told him to go home and write everything down—that way I would be able to check his information and find out if his story was true. I told him to do this, and to come back the next day. But I didn't think he would come back. And I also didn't think that if he did, he would bring the written account. Yet he did. He brought it the very next day."

"What was Ricardo like when he came?" I asked.

"He was always very correct with me. He talked slowly, humbly, with respect. He seemed very educated, poised, calm, and intelligent."

"And did he say that he wanted to turn himself in?"

"He said he wanted to be in a psychiatric hospital in New York."

"Did he say why he wanted to turn himself in?"

"Yes. He said that sometimes he became very worried and was afraid that he might kill again."

"Did he consider surrendering himself in Mexico?"

"No, he was afraid of something in Mexico."

I wish I could say that what Luquez went on to tell me about Mexico was in response to some other question of mine, that it was offered up because I am such a clever interviewer. But no, he was simply going on about arranging Ricardo's surrender when he said, "He told me he had had to run away from Mexico City. He gave me details, said that four policemen stopped him when he was in the airport there and held him and that he offered them money to let him go. He convinced them to stop at a bank. He gave them six thousand dollars and whatever he had in his pockets, except for his credit card and

passport. They got back in the car and then he realized they were going to hurt him because they were
taking him somewhere else and not where he wanted to go. So he attacked one of the guys—he knows
karate, you know—and they realized he was very
strong and could defend himself so they dropped
him off, and he ran back to the airport and bought
a ticket to Argentina."

I caught my breath. There it was, the story that
had been in *Clarín*—a story that had clearly originated with Ricardo! Had Luquez passed it along?
Had it been someone in his office? It didn't really
matter. What mattered was how this story of
Ricardo's tied together with everything else I'd
learned. There was what Susana had told Alberto,
that while working for some people in Mexico,
Ricardo had decided to part from his employers and
go into business on his own. There was what
Alberto had told me, that the people from whom
Ricardo had decided to part had the same kind of
power down there as the Mafia does in the States.
There was what Detective Hines had told me, that
Ricardo had claimed that these powerful bosses of
his were in the business of selling medical supplies—a business that had sounded suspiciously like
drugs to me. And now there was this tale, that
Ricardo, having struck out on his own in whatever
dangerous business it was in which he'd been
engaged, had been in fear for his life. All these bits
and pieces came together in my mind, and I felt I
had come to the end of my long quest, that I had
found the explanation for why Ricardo had turned
himself in.

I was elated by this, but I kept a bland expression
on my face, and Luquez went on talking, returning
now to the matter of his first encounter with
Ricardo. I barely listened. Ricardo *had* to turn him-

self in, my mind was racing, he had no choice—just as Elise McCarthy and John McGrath and so many other detectives who'd worked on the Caputo case had assumed. Ricardo *had* to turn himself in, he had no choice—and not because he was suddenly remorseful, but because he was suddenly being actively hunted by pursuers who were mightier and more merciless than those from whom he'd previously been hiding. No wonder he'd hightailed it out of Mexico. No wonder he'd surrendered. Sure, he'd figured he'd be sent to a psychiatric hospital, the kind of place from which he'd managed to escape in the past. But he must also have figured that no matter where he was sent, he'd be safe. Alive.

I didn't want Luquez to see my excitement. I asked him a few more questions. But my heart was no longer in conducting our interview, and in a few minutes I told him Alberto and I had to go. I didn't want to ask any more questions. I'd found what I'd been seeking all this time.

I left Mendoza for Buenos Aires the next day. I was eager to get back to New York and start writing my book. I would have flown home that very morning if there'd been a flight. But there wasn't one until the evening, and so I was forced to pass the day in Buenos Aires. What to do? I shopped for souvenirs, bought what tourists always bring home from Argentina, finely woven ponchos and silver maté cups. Then, stranded and not wanting to pass any more of my time just spending money, I rang up a few of the people whose names had been given me by friends in New York for just such an eventuality.

One such friend of a friend invited me to come visit him at his home. He was Emilio Mignone, a well-known human rights activist whose daughter had been abducted in 1976 by the military junta that had ruled Argentina at the time; she had not been seen or heard from since.

Mignone lived in a section of Buenos Aires I had not visited before, an area of cafés and old Parisian-looking apartment buildings. I took a creaky elevator up to a high floor in one of those buildings and was greeted by a distinguished-looking, bushy-eyebrowed man who appeared to be in his seventies but was youthfully dressed in a blue work shirt and jeans.

Mignone was a political man, still working hard to persuade the present Argentinian government to name and revoke its pardon of those who had tortured and murdered their fellow citizens during the country's infamous Dirty War. He filled me in on what was happening in Argentina now that President Menem had been reelected, told me about the stir that had been created by one Dirty War military officer who had recently confessed to tossing political prisoners to their death from official airplanes, and the fact that for the first time in their militaristic history, Argentinians were experiencing a revulsion against the armed forces and declining in droves to sign up for positions in officer training schools.

Then he asked me what had brought me to Argentina. I explained about Ricardo, but Mignone's eyes glazed over. His concerns were grander. And rightly so, for whereas Ricardo had murdered at least four and possibly six or eight or even a score of people, the Argentinian government during the Dirty War had murdered thousands.

Still, despite his having been dismissive of my project, I felt comfortable with Mignone. He reminded me of people I knew back home, people for whom politics is breath. And his apartment reminded me of the homes of several of my friends, a book-lined, plant-filled space hung with tapestries and warmed by a fireplace with a gas fire.

But on the mantelpiece was a photograph of a beautiful young girl, and I knew without asking that this must be Mignone's daughter, the girl who had "disappeared" so many years ago. It made me wonder if a part of Ricardo's viciousness had been forged not just in the coals of his own perverse psyche but in the national climate of violence in which he had been raised.

I brought this notion up with Mignone, who validated it. "A government that murders its own citizens is a breeding ground for all manner of individual cruelty," he said. But then, typically, he observed, "Still, it doesn't really matter how cruelty is bred, does it? What is important is how it is dealt with. It must not go unpunished."

What he was saying made me think immediately of how little punishment Ricardo had so far received for his crimes. He had been sentenced to eight and a third to twenty-five years for pleading guilty to manslaughter in the killing of Natalie Brown, a sentence that could, if he served just the minimum, see him out on the streets in a mere handful of years. And that was it, that was all, unless he got sentenced for murder in Westchester or San Francisco.

I hadn't thought about Ricardo's upcoming trials for weeks. I'd been too preoccupied with exploring his history, too focused on cause to think about resolution. Now, listening to Mignone, I felt a flare of curiosity about the pending trials. And when I left him to go to the airport, I realized that he had restored to me a certain lost balance and perspective, for as my taxi snaked through crowded rush-hour streets, I was no longer dwelling on Ricardo's past but on his future, on how our society would ultimately punish him.

17

When I returned to New York I paid an immediate visit to Jeanine Pirro's office up in Westchester County. She had by now assigned an assistant district attorney named Clem Patti to handle the prosecution of Ricardo for the murder of Judith Becker, and Patti was busily, but none too confidently, putting together his case. He was uneasy because his opponent, a legal aid attorney named Arlene Popkin, while not a star like Kennedy, nevertheless had a reputation as a formidable adversary. "She's planning to argue that Caputo was insane when he killed Becker," Patti, a handsome but dour-looking young man with a dark, brooding face, told me, "and while that's absurd, given what we know about him, you never can tell with juries. I mean, Ricardo *was* a patient in a mental hospital at the time he killed Becker."

We were sitting in Patti's office up at the Westchester County courthouse. The tiny space was filled with the usual clutter that marks the offices of junior district attorneys, the enormous notebooks and overstuffed cardboard boxes, the coffee-stained folders and stacks of unanswered message slips. Except for a couple of framed diplomas, there was

no sign of personal ownership other than a lone little carved wooden duck high up on a bookcase
crammed with law journals. Patti was not a man
who liked to be known.

He also didn't like talking to the press. But he
managed to open up long enough to tell me that
because of Popkin's plans, the prosecution had
begun testing Ricardo for a brain abnormality. "We
gave him an MRI," he said, "and we're probably
going to follow it up with something called a Nasal
Forensic Leads test. I don't think anything'll turn
up, but nowadays, when there's going to be an
insanity defense, you have to do all of this stuff. Just
in case the defense asks one of your psychiatric witnesses whether there are any tests that could have
been done to establish that a defendant has brain
disease and the witness says yes. Costs a fortune."

"Well, maybe Ricardo will plead guilty again," I
ventured, to lift Patti's spirits. "Maybe he'll cop out
like he did in Nassau County."

"Maybe," Patti glowered. "But I doubt it. I imagine his family wants him to take a shot at a trial."

"I don't think so," I said, and told him about my
trip to Argentina. Patti was fascinated and surprised
that I'd been able to interview Ricardo's family.
"Well, I guess it's because I got to know the brother,"
I offered.

"Alberto? You mean *he* talked to you?"

"Yeah."

"I'm amazed. He wouldn't talk to us. To our
police. Not back when Judith Becker was murdered
and we were trying to find Ricardo."

"That was a long time ago. I think Alberto has
changed a lot since then."

Alberto. While we were still in Argentina, we'd
discussed the information Luquez had given us

about Ricardo's flight from Mexico, and during that conversation Alberto had looked at me with a jaundiced expression and said, "It figures. It never made sense that Ricardo would just turn himself in out of the clear blue." But we'd never talked about whether he thought Ricardo should plead guilty in the murder of Judith Becker or hold out for a trial. And now that we were both back home, I made a date to visit him up in Riverdale again and discuss the matter with him.

His position was pretty much what I'd anticipated it might be when I talked to Patti. "Have Ricardo go to trial? Why would I want that? The only thing a trial'll do is create more pain for the Becker family. And for me and my family, too."

The serenely beautiful Kim was sitting across from us, just as she'd been when I'd first come to their home and Alberto had told me the story of his parents and childhood. And just as she'd been on that day, she was quiet, letting her husband do most of the talking. "Of course, I can't tell Ricardo what to do, can I?" he was saying. "It's up to him. But he knows how I feel. I just want him to get the thing over and done with."

"And you?" I said to Kim, wanting to include her. Besides, I really was curious as to how she, who had written the couple's original apologia for Ricardo, the press release in which she'd taken society to task for leaving her brother-in-law "alone with his disease," felt about him now.

She lowered her gaze and answered me indirectly in that high-pitched, childlike voice of hers. "Since I first met Ricardo, my husband's pain, my child's confusion, and my own anger and shame have done nothing but grow. Did Alberto ever tell you about the time he was away in Australia and Ricardo called me up?"

She looked over at Alberto, who shook his head.

"Well, Ricardo called me from jail," Kim singsonged. "He said his wife was in town. Up from Mexico. And that he wanted me to put her up. He called me five times about it. And one of the times, he said the most awful things. Said he'd gotten out of jail and gone to a hotel with his wife. Said they tried to screw, but he couldn't do it because she looked repulsive, all swollen and hideous. I didn't know what to think and I called Kennedy in a panic, and he called the jail and we found out it was all just a story."

"Some story," I said.

"Yes," she sighed, her voice belying the indignation that resided in her words. "Yes. And why tell it to me? And why just then, when he knew Alberto was out of town?"

Kim didn't come out and say that she felt Ricardo had been toying with her, or that he'd scared the life—and the idealism—out of her. She was too circuitous a person for that, too bent on maintaining an aura of calm. But it was clear to me that the brother-in-law she had once seen as society's neglected victim was no longer someone she cared much about urging to go to trial.

But there was still Arlene Popkin. She was still hoping to come up with some neurophysiological evidence that might enable her to persuade a jury that Ricardo belonged in a mental hospital, not a prison. And to that end, after Ricardo received the brain abnormality test Patti had mentioned to me and it failed to show any noticeable brain disease, she had begun trying to find a neuropsychiatrist with better equipment than that which had so far been used to study Ricardo.

I'd met Popkin, had spoken to her briefly when

she'd come to one of Ricardo's court sessions in
Nassau. She'd struck me as an intense and ideolog-
ical woman, passionate about her role as a public
defender, and passionate, too, in the defiant unfash-
ionableness of her dress. Unlike most of the women
lawyers I knew, who went to court in high heels, fit-
ted suits, and chic haircuts, she'd been wearing flats
and a long, shapeless dress, and her graying, wavy
hair had flowed thick and loose past her shoulders.

Popkin was certain Ricardo was insane, and one
of her reasons, she told me when I telephoned her
now about the Westchester case, was that "he isn't
really a violent man."

"Huh?" I said rudely.

"Yes, he has used excessive horrific violence, but
on *discrete* occasions. As far as I can see, he doesn't
get into fistfights. He doesn't spank his children. He
doesn't display uncontrollable anger—I mean, take
that incident in El Paso, when he put a weapon to
the neck of a guard. He didn't do more than scratch
the man. If he were truly a violent individual, he
would have cut him severely. But he didn't. Because
he's not a violent man. He's just a man who kills on
some occasions."

"Quite a few occasions," I muttered. "By his own
account."

"There are all kinds of physiological abnormalities that can spark occasional violence," Popkin said,
and, sounding like the optimistic Dr. Linares in
Mendoza, trilled, "structural abnormalities, chemi-
cal abnormalities, electrical abnormalities. In addi-
tion, there are all sorts of tests to detect them.
NMRs. CAT scans. PET scans. Spinal fluid analyses."

I daresay Popkin could have presented some
interesting arguments, but she never got the chance.
Toward the end of June, Ricardo did decide to plead

guilty. But neither of the lawyers seemed to know why. Patti thought it might be because if he did, he had a shot at a lesser sentence. "The maximum for murder is twenty-five to life," Patti explained, "the minimum, fifteen to life. A plea, depending of course on the judge, could net him something on the low end of the sentence." Popkin thought it was because Ricardo didn't want to cause any further suffering. "He's a man with a conscience," she insisted.

Neither explanation made much sense to me. I felt certain that no judge, once having read the detailed account of Ricardo's history that the prosecution was sure to file before the sentencing, would offer Ricardo the low end of the scale, and I doubted that Ricardo was a man of conscience. So I called Alberto to see if he knew what had prompted the sudden plea. But, "Beats me," Alberto said. He had been visiting Ricardo in jail regularly ever since he'd been moved from Nassau to Westchester. "Maybe that lawyer of his told him she didn't have anything much to go on."

"You think?"

"Don't know why else. Not that he'd ever tell me. Whenever I ask him about something important, something I want to know, he just makes a kind of pouting face, like a baby, and shrugs his shoulders."

Several weeks later Ricardo was taken from his jail cell to a large, sterile courtroom in the Westchester County courthouse to learn his second sentence. He looked different from the way he had on the day of his sentencing in Natalie Brown's killing, looked heavier, paler, less kempt. His hair had gotten long, his cheeks were hairy with sideburns that gave him the disheveled aspect of a nineteenth-century *bandito*, and although Alberto and

Kim had sent him a jacket and white shirt to wear,
he had eschewed them, donning instead a casual
yellow T-shirt.

I suppose this was fitting, for all in all, the proceedings were far less formal, or at least less filled
with pomp and circumstance, than they had been
on the day he was sentenced for what he'd done to
Natalie Brown. Fewer reporters were present, and
the speeches of the lawyers were shorter and less
ardent than they had been at the earlier sentencing.

But Judith's mother, Jane Becker, and her sister,
Janie, had come to court, dressed in their
Connecticut-matron floral prints, polished white
sandals, and pearls, and Janie, who also made a
speech, was every bit as moving as Ed Brown had
been months before. "My sister, Judith Becker, was
murdered by Ricardo Caputo in October of 1974,"
she said. "With my sister's violent death, I lost my
only sibling and my parents suffered the devastating
death of their child. Unfortunately, there are no adequate words to describe the emotions I felt, nor the
scars that, although this happened so long ago, still
remain with me and my family and will remain with
us for the rest of our lives."

As she spoke, reading her words from a prepared
statement, Janie's hands began to tremble. And soon
the paper she held between them was shaking like a
leaf in a windstorm. But she plowed ahead:
"Ricardo Caputo has a personality capable of
manipulating and using anyone for his own bene-
fits. I say this having met him once, albeit briefly.
He appeared to be an articulate, charming young
man. And herein lies the tremendous danger he presents to us all, even today.

"He has a personality capable of manipulating
anyone. If these tactics fail, he is more than capable
of murder. If there is anyone able to be viewed as a

menace to society, it should be him. And I beg the court to sentence him to the most severe penalty allowable by law."

Ricardo, who knew Janie, who had once instructed her in the merits of various Argentinian wines, avoided her gaze. He sat stiffly, morosely, eyes on the judge. And when he was asked if he had anything to say in his own defense, he volunteered only, "I want to say that I'm sorry for what I did. I was sick when I did it. I was in the hospital and unfortunately I couldn't help myself."

The judge, Kenneth H. Lange, thanked him coolly and coolly began his own oration. "This was no simple crime of passion. You beat and strangled Judith Becker. But you also took her keys, her pocketbook, her credit cards, and her car. Judith Becker's death devastated her parents and her sister, but there was also a real sense of loss among her colleagues and even among the patients in the penal institution where she worked. This devoted person, Judith Becker, was a bright young woman who had studied hard to prepare for a career as a psychologist. She apparently saw some good in you, Mr. Caputo, and she went out of her way to improve your life as an inmate in the correction system that she served. Perhaps her inexperience led her to discount the risk that you would do to her what you had already done to Natalie Brown. But you did it and went on to commit other murders."

Lange then delivered his sentence: the maximum, twenty-five years to life, to run consecutively with the sentence of eight and a third to twenty-five years that Ricardo had already received for killing Natalie Brown. Ricardo, it was apparent, would be an old man before he saw the outside of a prison—and he hadn't even been sentenced yet for killing Barbara Taylor.

*   *   *

Alberto had stayed away from the sentencing, even though the Westchester courthouse was only a few minutes from his home. I took that as an indication that in some major way, he was washing his hands of his brother. Yet he was still going to visit him, still bringing him packages of food and clothing, as I discovered in a telephone call several days later. It was a call I made, to let Alberto know what had transpired at the sentencing. But it could just as well have been one he made to me, for ever since my trip to Argentina, he and I had been calling each other regularly, sometimes to convey information, sometimes just to check in, rather as if we were friends. And I suppose that's what we were, our discoveries in Mendoza about Ricardo having created a bond between us, one that our spouses, for all their interest in what we'd learned, didn't quite share. More, Alberto and I had gotten into the habit of complaining to each other—he about how unresponsive he felt Ricardo was or how onerous it was to have to visit him, me about the difficulties I was experiencing now that I was starting to write my book—and I've often felt that what lies at the heart of friendship is the chance to exchange grumbles, that our friends are the people to whom we feel free to complain.

"I'm going to see Ricardo next week," Alberto said to me on this particular occasion. "Though he never has anything to say to me. And I've got nothing to say to him. We sit there like two lumps."

I'd heard that before. And I suggested something I'd suggested before. "So don't go."

"No, I have to. I promised my mother I'd look in on him from time to time."

That was the end of that, but a few days later, we had another phone conversation. "I'm going to see

Ricardo tomorrow," Alberto said this time. "Why don't you come with me? I hate going alone."

"Why don't you ask Kim?" In all the months I'd been investigating the Caputo case, I'd never tried to obtain an interview with Ricardo. At the beginning, I'd thought it would be pointless. I'd made it clear to his lawyer that I'd undertaken my book because I knew Jacqui Bernard and that I had little sympathy for his client. He'd never have allowed Ricardo to see me. Later on, after Kennedy dropped out of the case and I had gotten to know Alberto, my feelings had grown more complicated. I was trying to sort them out when Alberto replied, "I've asked Kim. She doesn't want to go."

"Me either," I admitted.

"Why not? I'd have thought you'd leap at the chance."

"I don't know. I'm afraid, I guess."

"Of what? Of prisons?"

"No, I've been to see any number of prisoners. This is different."

"Then what are you afraid of? Him? He's not getting out."

I had the phone in one hand, a pencil in the other. But I put the pencil down and began to rub my forehead, which had started to throb. "It isn't that I'm afraid of Ricardo," I said, not sure if I was telling the truth. "I think it's more subtle than that. I think I'm afraid that if I meet him, the picture of him I've built up in my mind will alter, and I won't be able to write the book. Either that, or I'm afraid I might like him."

"Oh, that," Alberto said. "Well, yes, you're a woman, so there's always that."

18

But of course, I did go. On a sweltering summer's morning when the murky sky overhead seemed clamped down like the lid of a stone-gray coffin, I took a taxi up to Riverdale, then drove with Alberto to the Westchester County jail. It was situated, ironically, in the idyllically named town of Valhalla, New York, and unlike the other prisons I'd visited, it wasn't a massive and stolid structure with the look of a human warehouse. Rather, it was low and sprawling, a red-brick, tile-trimmed building that appeared on first sight to be cheerful, a suburban medical center rather than a place of confinement.

Once we passed through the doors, however, all resemblance to a less fearsome establishment ceased. We were greeted in a dimly lit entranceway by burly guards, directed peremptorily to stash our money and keys and even our jackets in a dilapidated locker, and barkingly instructed to enter our names and the name of the prisoner we wanted to see in a large battered register that looked like a relic from Dickensian days.

I had not applied for permission to enter the jail as a journalist; there hadn't been time to make that application and receive the approval of the warden.

Instead, I wrote down, although the inscription gave me pause, that I was a friend of prisoner number 28176 and surrendered my notebook and pens. Then Alberto and I were passed through an electronic security machine, one apparently far more sensitive than those used in airports, for we had to remove our watches and even our eyeglasses, after which we were passed through a door that did not clang shut, as the doors of the other prisons I'd visited did, but which closed just as ominously, making a tremendous whooshing sound.

I felt claustrophobic, and we weren't even all the way inside yet. We were in a holding area, waiting to be okayed by yet other guards, who were too preoccupied with a hysterical woman demanding the right to bring cookies with her to pay any attention to us. We cooled our heels for a long time, Alberto quieter than I had ever known him to be. Then at last the woman with the cookies abandoned her efforts to bend the rules, and we were sent through another whooshing door to the visiting room.

Noise was what greeted us: a grinding, overpowering noise. About forty little tables were in the modestly air-conditioned room, and each was occupied by a jumpsuited prisoner and three or four friends and relatives, many of them with babies in their arms, and the din of conversation and squalling was colossal. How would I ever be able to hear whatever it was that Ricardo might say to me? I wondered. And then, *would* he say anything? Alberto had informed him that he was bringing me and explained that I was writing a book about him, and Ricardo had raised no objections. But now, waiting as a guard looked for an empty table for me and Alberto, I was filled with doubts. "Are you sure he said it was okay to bring me?" I asked Alberto, speaking loudly so that he could hear me.

"Yes," he shouted.

"And you told him I was writing about him?" I bellowed.

"Yes," he bellowed back.

The guard, saving his vocal chords, used his chin to gesture at the table he wanted us to take. Mercifully, it was in a relatively quiet corner.

Still, to hear one another, Alberto and I had to sit far forward in our chairs, and I realized that to make out whatever Ricardo might say to me, I was going to have to sit close to him. That, and to try to memorize whatever he said. Both were unhappy prospects, but I didn't have time to brood about them for, a moment later, Ricardo arrived and plunked himself down on a chair between us.

He looked terrible. He was dressed in a jaunty yellow jumpsuit, but his cheeks and chin were bristling with stubble, his sparse hair was plastered sweatily to his forehead, and his brown eyes were bloodshot and ringed with large dark circles. "Sorry I couldn't shave," he said, "but they limit your shaves. Showers, too. Even though it's like an oven inside."

Alberto was uncharitable. "I can tell you didn't shower. You smell, man."

But Ricardo didn't seem to mind. He made the pouting expression Alberto had once described to me and shrugged his shoulders.

So far he'd said nothing directly to me, but now he turned and said, "Alberto says you know all about me. That true?"

"Hardly."

"Yeah, well, there's a lot to know." He stared at me cheekily, appraisingly. "I'm an interesting fellow, right?"

Was he flirting with me? Trying to impress me? It seemed that way, and to avoid his gaze, I cast my eyes down and studied his arms and hands, which were sprawled across the table. The arms were hairless and pasty white, and the hands were extraordinarily small, a phenomenon I found strange in view of all the damage he'd caused with them.

"They say I'm a charmer," he went on teasingly. "What do you say? You find me charming?"

If he was coming on to me, there was something disconcertingly crude about the way he was going about it. Something hostile, too. And although I'd been worried that I might succumb to Ricardo's much-touted ability to charm, I realized at this moment that I faced no such danger. If he had ever truly had that ability—and his behavior was making me wonder if what I'd heard about him wasn't all myth—he had lost it by now, lost it along with his once-trim figure and smiling good looks. "I don't know you yet," I said coldly.

"But you want to, right?" Once again, he gave me that creepy sexual stare, and leaning close to him the way I was, hanging on his lips, his words, I suddenly experienced his evil energy. It was trying to draw me into his orbit. I felt it, I swear.

"Linda wants to ask you some questions," Alberto, businesslike, broke the silence that had descended among us.

"Yeah? Like what kind of questions?"

I felt hostile, too. You killed Jacqui Bernard, didn't you, was what I wanted to say, like some TV cop. But I knew I was going to have to defuse the tension between us before I could get to the subject of Jacqui. Or any controversial subject. So although I'd seen nothing particularly commendable about Ricardo, at least thus far, I decided to flatter him, and I told him what a brave thing he'd done in pleading guilty to Judith Becker's murder. "You spared her mother. That was a good thing to do."

He nodded, relishing the image of himself as a noble figure. "I'm not a bad man, whatever you've heard. I'm a sick man."

"Yes, of course," I agreed, and as I did believe that anyone who could commit as many murders as Ricardo had was sick, in the soul if not in the legal sense of the word, I had no trouble sounding sincere. This was fortunate, for although he continued to stare at me, there was far less hostility in his glance than there had been earlier, so little that, a moment later, I asked him to begin our interview by telling me about the time he'd been raped as a child. I knew it was a subject that would allow him to present himself in another favorable guise, that of sufferer, victim.

"I was a little kid," he began, speaking slowly at first and then warming to his account. "And the guy who did it to me was in his thirties. He'd run into me on the street a few times, and each time, he'd given me candy. This time, he invited me into his house, and he gave me chocolate. I remember it was chocolate. Then suddenly he lowered my pants and grabbed me from behind and stuck it in. I wanted to get away, but he held on to me. I couldn't move. I couldn't breathe."

I felt sorry for him. I'd have felt sorry for anyone who'd had, or even imagined he'd had, that experience. "It must have been awful for you," I said without too much difficulty.

"Yeah, terrible. You don't know how terrible." He was reveling in self-pity, his bloodshot eyes seeming to grow even redder.

"What happened afterward? How did you get away?"

"The guy let me go. He said that if I told anyone what he'd done, he'd hurt me, and he let me go. I ran out and then I walked home very slowly, and

when I got there, I went to the bathroom and saw
there was blood on my buttocks. I didn't understand
what had happened. I was only seven. But I knew
something had happened to me."

Something profound, he was implying.
Something that had somehow turned him into a
murderer. I didn't buy it. Wasn't even entirely certain that he *had* been raped, given the things Dr.
Padin had told me in Mendoza about his constant
lies, and the way early sexual abuse has become, in
our time, every criminal's excuse for his own abu-
sive activities. But I managed not to communicate
my doubt, and my effort at concealment paid off.
Ricardo proceeded from telling me about the rape
to talking about how, two years later when he was
nine, he was still feeling so miserable that he almost
killed himself.

"It was at that sleepaway school my mother and
Luis sent me to. I had just received Communion and
I was standing on a balcony, watching some priests
who were down below, singing or chanting or something. And I thought, 'Now I'm pure, I can go to
heaven with no sins,' and I leaned over the balcony
and tried to throw myself down. But I couldn't do it.
Maybe it would have been better if I had. You
think?"

I knew it would have been politic to say no, to
offer him a few comforting clichés along the lines
Alicia might have tendered, things like "Life is best"
and "Suicide is against God's law." But I couldn't
bring myself to do it, and I said, "Yes. Maybe it
would have been better."

"You're a tough one," he said, and I thought,
Damn, I should have handled that better. Now he's
going to clam up. But to my surprise, when I
ignored his remark and suggested that now we talk
about his adolescence, he went on speaking. I guess

that by then he was basking in receiving attention, even negative attention.

He told me about his fights with Luis, his hospitalization—"it was for depression," he insisted—and his involvement with a neo-fascist group in Mendoza. "They had meetings, taught you judo and gave you sandwiches. I liked it, but then they wanted me to go out on an action, stand in front of the local synagogue and shout insults at the Jews as they came out. I didn't want to do it. I hate that kind of thing. And I quit the group."

It was an odd story in view of the fact that Alberto had told me that Ricardo had been apolitical as an adolescent, and I suspected that he'd told it, perhaps even made it up right there on the spot, because he was still trying to find a way to impress me. I knew that Alberto had informed him that I was Jewish.

Still, it was an interesting story, and if Ricardo's purpose was to court favor with me, he'd found a cleverer way of going about it than his earlier crude efforts at flirtation. Indeed, I felt I was witnessing at last the kind of shrewdness with which he had insinuated himself into the good graces of his victims, the way he'd made a practice of telling them things they wanted to hear and wanted to believe about him.

A while later, after some further, not very fruitful, discussion of his adolescence, I asked him to tell me about the women he'd killed. He did, describing how he'd met them and, invariably, telling me that each had allowed him to take her to bed on their first or second date. He also claimed that each of them had loved him to distraction and, interestingly, attributed that love almost solely to his sexual prowess.

The twenty-year-old Natalie, he told me, as he'd

told Dr. Dietz, had had a great many lovers before she met him, but they hadn't been any good. "Just young kids, mostly. I was young, too, but I'd been going to whores for years. I knew what I was doing. That was why she loved me."

The popular Barbara, he related, had never been able to have an orgasm with a man before he came along, and that had made her devoted to him. "I was the only one who could get her to come. She used to use a vibrator on herself, but she didn't have to with me. And that made her adore me."

The idealistic Judith, he said, had loved him because he had allowed her to express the secret side of herself, the one that liked pain and humiliation during sex.

Only the wealthy Laura Gomez had been a little bit different. She, too, had loved him for his sexuality. But she'd also loved him "because we were so alike. Both of us were the neglected children in our families."

I listened to all this with my most professional demeanor, remembering how Dietz had listened to him. Coolly, nonreactively. Then I gradually led him to the subject of the murders. He showed no resistance, indeed talked openly about them, but he told me nothing new, insisting on the explanation I had already heard him offer to Dr. Dietz: that there was no premeditation, only a sudden and overpowering urge to kill inspired by visual and auditory delusions. "I *loved* Natalie," he said. "Why would I have wanted to kill her? I loved Laura, too. Barbara I didn't love, but she was my friend. I liked her a lot. The only one I didn't love or like was Judith. With her, it was more a matter of need. I needed her."

Still, for all his protestations about having felt love, friendship, or need for the women he'd admitted killing, it was apparent that he hadn't respected

them, had felt he had won them too swiftly. This
became evident a while later when I got him to talk
about the women in his life whom he *hadn't* killed.
The women he'd married. "Susi," he said, referring
approvingly to his current wife, "was a virgin when
I met her, and she wouldn't have sex with me until
we were married." And "Felicia," he said, referring
admiringly to his first wife, the one who'd disappeared in the early 1980s "made me wait until two
weeks after we met." Talking about Felicia brought
out in him an emotionality that had been lacking
when he'd spoken of the other women, including
Susi. He smiled—it was the only time that day that
I saw him smile—when he told me that on the night
he first met Felicia, they'd danced a glorious tango
together. And he half-closed his eyes and looked
genuinely sad when he told me about their first
date. "She said, 'I don't know anything about you.
Who are you? For all I know, you're the Hillside
Strangler.' And in a way I was. But I couldn't tell her
that, could I?"

I went past the question. I was interested in the
distinction he'd made just before between the
women he'd killed, all of whom he'd said had gone
to bed with him right after meeting him, and the
women he'd married, both of whom had insisted on
a waiting period for sex. "Do you think the fact that
Felicia and Susi didn't go to bed with you right
away was what kept them safe from you?" I asked.
"Do you think you might have wanted to kill Natalie
and Judith and the others because they were so sexually free?"

The assumption seemed an obvious one to me,
especially given what I knew to be Ricardo's fury at
Alicia for *her* sexual appetites, but Ricardo, perhaps
to curry favor with me, acted as if I'd just offered
him a rare and subtle bit of wisdom. "That's inter-

esting," he said, nodding and dramatically wrinkling his excessively high forehead. "I hadn't thought of it before. But maybe you're right. Maybe it's true."

That was the closest I came that day to getting Ricardo to say anything about the murders that he hadn't said before, hadn't proffered to Kennedy and Dietz. More, the momentary insight he seemed to have gained had no staying power. Toward the end of our visit, he returned to insisting that there was no rational explanation for the murders. "I don't know why I killed those women," he said. And then, giving voice to his true delusion: "Because I'm not that kind of person. Because basically, I'm a good person."

By then, a guard had come to our table and indicated that the visiting period was about to end. I realized with dismay that I hadn't asked Ricardo about Jacqui Bernard, and that if I was going to do so, I would have to come back another time. Right now, it was too late. He was on his feet, as disciplined as a soldier, and moving toward the entrance to the cells without so much as the wave or backward glance in which other prisoners were indulging.

"He's so cold," I said to Alberto.

"Yes"—he nodded—"that's my baby brother."

I saw Ricardo two more times, once again at the Valhalla jail and once at the Downstate Correctional Facility in Fishkill, New York, to which he was soon transferred to await a final prison assignment.

For these visits, I had time to do a little more preparation. I called John McGrath, Gordon McEwan's partner, and asked him, as an experienced detective, to give me some tips about how to get Ricardo to be more forthcoming. I hadn't spoken to McGrath in a number of months, but he was nevertheless eager to be of help.

"Start by getting his side of the story," he suggested. "And build up his ego."

I said I'd instinctually done pretty much just that.

"Well, do it some more, and then come at him from left field. I mean, if you want to ask him about Jacqui Bernard, don't just pop out with it. Say, 'You must have had a hard time, being an immigrant and all. Did anyone ever try to help you get a visa?' Or, 'Did anyone ever loan you a car?' We know from the informant that Jacqui did those things for him, but you act like you just came up with them out of the blue."

I said I'd ask those questions, and then I called Inspector Sanders in San Francisco. He and I had talked frequently in the months since I'd been out to see him. I'd even told him about my trip to Argentina, a report that had prompted him to assume his professorial mode and say, "I just *knew* the mother played a role in getting Caputo to turn himself in. I always tell my students, when you want a black or Hispanic guy to surrender, you gotta get to the mother. He'll listen to her. With Asian guys, it's the father. With white guys, forget it. They don't have the same kind of feelings about their parents." Now, I told him I'd been to see Caputo, which elicited from him an exuberant, "Boy, I wish I could have been there. Just a little speck on the wall. There's a lot of questions I'd have liked to ask him."

"You might not have gotten the answers you wanted. He's pretty cagey."

"Of course. How in hell would he have kept himself hidden for twenty years if he wasn't."

Sanders was planning to let Caputo settle into the New York State prison system, then extradite him to California for a first hearing in the murder of

Barbara Taylor. "We'll probably be coming for him in six weeks or thereabouts. So if you're going to see him again, you better go soon."

"Thanks for telling me. I will. And meanwhile, do you have any tips for me? Any suggestions about *how* to question him?"

"Just be friendly. Get him talking."

"I did. And he told me some interesting things. But mostly, he was banal."

"End of story," Sanders said. "Most murderers are banal. It's just their crimes that are interesting."

For my second visit, the one to Valhalla, I applied for permission to enter the jail as a journalist, which would have allowed me to take notes and interview Ricardo in a private area. But after first granting me the permission I sought, a police captain at the jail called back and told me it wouldn't be possible. "We've checked with the inmate," he said, "and he doesn't want to see you." This puzzled me, for Ricardo and I had parted perfectly amicably the last time. And when the captain went on to say, "This Caputo is a very dangerous man, and we don't want to have the responsibility if anything happens to you," I figured that that was the real reason I was being denied the permission I sought, and that most likely the jail authorities had not even bothered to check if Ricardo wanted to see me.

This proved to be the case. I went up to the jail— alone this time, as Alberto hadn't wanted to pay another visit to his baby brother so soon after the last one—logged in once again as a friend of prisoner 28176, was assigned a table in the visiting room, and shortly was greeted by a swift-moving Ricardo, who was not only glad to see me, but who this time offered his hand in greeting.

That little hand, extended toward me, gave me

the willies. But I took it and shook it, wondering if the grip would add something to my knowledge of the man. It didn't. Ricardo's fingers grasped mine loosely, perfunctorily. Whatever power resided in that hand, Ricardo had decided not to reveal it.

He had also decided not to reveal himself this time in anything but his victim role. In response to my asking why his parents had sent him to the sleepaway school at which he'd contemplated suicide, he explained that the children at the school he had previously attended were always making fun of him. "I was crazy, but to the kids I knew, crazy was a joke, something to laugh at." In response to a question about his adolescence, he told me that Luis had thrown him out of the house, whereupon he'd been picked up by a doctor who had taken him to a park and offered him money if he'd let him have anal sex with him. "I did it, but it brought back all the memories of the time I'd been raped," he said mournfully, "and afterward, I felt so bad that I went back to my house and stole a gun from Luis and put it to my head and cocked the trigger."

I was deeply into my own role, that of sympathetic listener, and I shook my head in dismay, the way one does when someone describes a suicide attempt. So it was Ricardo again, not me, who said, "Maybe it would have been better if I'd pulled that trigger. Others wouldn't have had to die." I agreed gently, cautiously, and he said, "And I wouldn't have had to suffer the way I did."

This spurred him to flood me with tales of the miseries he had endured, starting with his earliest days in the States. "I had to work two jobs. I worked all day washing walls in one hotel, then all night cleaning floors in another. And people made fun of my accent. Treated me like scum. Because I was a Latino."

Was this what he had told Jacqui Bernard? If he had, it would have affected her deeply. For myself, I was impervious. My apparent softness and concern for him was a performance as devious as his own. We were two actors on a stage.

I didn't like my part very much, but he seemed to be enjoying his. "Only Natalie," he was going on, "only Natalie took an interest in me in those days. That's why I loved her so much."

"But then she decided to break up with you," I said, still trying to sound sympathetic. "I guess that disappointed you. Made you upset."

"No," he said firmly. "Natalie never wanted to break up with me."

I was tired of the play we were enacting and I decided it was time to become more confrontational. "But you told the police back when you killed her that she told you she was seeing another man."

Ricardo opened his eyes wide, then made the pouting expression Alberto had once described to me and shook his head. "No, no, I never said that."

"And Judith, didn't she decide to break up with you?"

Again, he shook his head.

"But Judith told you she had a new boyfriend. A policeman. That must have made you angry."

"No. She'd told me about him a while before I killed her. I'd gotten over it. I know the prosecutor told my lawyer that they have a witness who heard me and Judith quarreling on the night I killed her, but that's wrong. We didn't quarrel. We had supper. I went to the bathroom. And I came out and killed her."

"And Barbara?"

"Same thing."

His denials made me remember the story Alberto had told me about how when he was a boy, Ricardo had been observed taunting a ram, only to insist, despite the accounts of those who had witnessed his behavior, that he had never done such a thing. As a result, I didn't mention that Inspector Sanders had told me that he, too, had a witness who had also overheard a quarrel—this one on the night Barbara was killed. What was the point? Ricardo was clearly going to stick to the story he liked best, no matter what anyone else said. Still, I asked him about Laura, just to cover all the bases. "And you had no reason for killing Laura?"

"None. She loved me, too. Though sometimes I think that the reason I killed her was that I wanted to put an end to her suffering. You see, she loved me and wanted to marry me. And I knew I couldn't marry her. I was a killer. I couldn't tell her that. She'd never have understood. So I couldn't marry her. But when I said I couldn't, she got very unhappy. And I wanted to end her pain, her longing for me."

"You beat her with an iron bar to put an end to her pain?" I said, incredulous.

"Yes," he allowed, straight-faced. "Yes, that's right."

I'd never asked questions of a psychopathic liar before. It gave me the feeling that I was trying to clamber up a mountain with slopes so sheer that it was impossible to gain even a toehold. And I fell silent, as exhausted as if I'd actually been climbing.

But Ricardo was still enjoying himself. Without prompting, he began describing how difficult his life had been after he'd killed Laura. "The police were hunting me like I was a dog," he said, his voice full of pathos. "I had to flee from place to place, always looking over my shoulder, always having to hide, always having to pretend I was someone else. And I couldn't even look for a decent job. I had to be a waiter, all the time a waiter, because people don't really look at waiters. Once, when I was living in Cicero, though, I thought I could make something of my life by opening a restaurant. I'd learned to make stocks and soups, and I thought, I'll open a little place of my own. I even went looking for a spot and found the perfect one. A place where there'd been a restaurant before. But I couldn't do it. I was afraid if I opened a restaurant, I'd have to get permits, and the police would get wind of me. So I just went on working for other people. And taking my lumps. Getting ordered about. Pushed around. A Latino in the United States. Here without a visa."

I felt this was as good a chance as any I was likely to get to ask the questions John McGrath had suggested, the questions that might lead Ricardo to say something about Jacqui Bernard. So I interrupted him and said, "And in all that time, was no one ever kind to you? Did no one ever offer to help you out with Immigration? Lend you money? Loan you a car?"

He was way ahead of me. "No," he shook his head sadly. "No one. No one ever offered to help me."

"I'm not getting anything out of him," I complained to my husband that night. "Just lies and self-pity."

"That's not nothing," he said supportively. "You're getting *him.*"

"I suppose. But I'm finding it hard to understand what all those women saw in him."

"I guess they believed his lies. They didn't know all you know about him. And I guess they thought they could make him stop feeling so sad and sorry for himself."

"I guess."

"But why don't you ask *him* what they saw in him. I always ask something like that when I'm doing a psychiatric consultation. At the very least, you'll learn what *he* considers the secret of his success."

"That's good," I said. "I'll try it."

My third visit to Ricardo took place at the Downstate Correctional Facility in Fishkill, New York. This time, once again, I went with Alberto, and after a long drive, we found ourselves in an even more modern prison, this one with an airy visiting room that, with its color-coordinated chartreuse tables and dark green chairs and its gleaming machines dispensing soft drinks and snacks, reminded us of a school cafeteria. When Ricardo arrived in the room, he ignored me and fell immediately into an intense conversation with Alberto. "Last night," he told him emotionally, "I realized there is no God. We are alone here. I am alone. God doesn't exist. I'm sure of this now and I'm feeling like a fool because all this time, I've been going down on my knees and praying to Him. Like Mami told me to do."

"What happened last night?" Alberto asked.

"Mami let me down. I got a letter from my wife and she told me she hasn't heard a word from Mami. She went back on her word. She promised to support Susi, and she hasn't done it."

"But Mami has no money," Alberto said soothingly. "You know that."

"I'm not talking about financial support," Ricardo exploded. "I'm talking about moral support. She promised me. But she lied."

"She's getting on," Alberto reminded him. "She's not the woman she used to be."

"I don't care," Ricardo fumed. "She promised. It's because of her that I lost my faith."

In his rage at his mother, he sounded like a two-year-old. He was having a tantrum, a shouting, blaming, irrational tantrum.

I was glad to be outside the conversation, to let it swirl past me. But soon, Ricardo tried to involve me. "You know, when I went to Argentina," he said, turning toward me, "I went there with the intention of killing my mother and Luis. I wanted them dead. The two of them. That's why I went home."

I looked at him with a deadpan expression, but the fact of the matter was that I couldn't believe my ears. He had always maintained that he had gone to Argentina with the intention of turning himself in. Had that been a lie? And was this the truth? It was impossible to be sure, but as he continued to speak, I began to think he was at last being honest with me. "I was sick of my life," he said, his lips a vivid red slash across his white face. "And it was all their fault. My mother's especially. She never loved me. She just said she did. She was always lying. Pretending. And I thought that if I killed her, I could stop hating her for lying about loving me."

Was that why he had killed all the other women? Because he was convinced when they tried to break up with him that they had lied about loving him? I didn't ask that question. I was too frightened of his rage. I just let him rant on, until finally, the energy beginning to drain from his voice, he said, "I was going to kill her, but in the end, I didn't. My mother looked so pitiful and small and I couldn't do it."

"Poor Mami," Alberto sighed.

"Sometimes I'm sorry I didn't do it," Ricardo said.

But his tantrum was subsiding. And soon, he fell silent, and I felt able to talk to him once again. "How would you have killed your mother?" I asked, wondering if he'd actually had a plan. "Did you have a weapon?"

"I don't need a weapon," he replied scathingly. "I was going to do it with my bare hands."

He was quite calm after that, as if voicing his fury and his thwarted plan had given him a kind of peace. He even suggested that Alberto buy him a cheeseburger from one of the machines. And while he ate, wolfing down his burger hungrily, he made small talk, told us about his routine in jail, one hour for playing baseball, one hour for watching TV. "We always have fights over what to watch," he said. "Me, I like *Baywatch*. All those girls!"

This led him to reminisce about the days he'd lived in Hawaii and roamed the beaches picking up women. "My body was great then," he said nostalgically. "I was very fit and very tan, and when I walked along the water, I could feel all the girls looking at me. I could have had any one of them I wanted."

"You certainly did attract some remarkable women," I said, remembering the question my husband had suggested I ask. "I mean, really accomplished and beautiful women."

"Yeah"—he smiled—"like Laura. She was the best-looking. And the richest."

Talking about Laura didn't fill him with regrets. In fact, it made him hungry. "Get me another cheeseburger," he said to Alberto, who rose oblig-ingly just as I asked, "What do you think it was about you that drew such wonderful women to you?"

"I was charming. I told you that."

Alberto headed for the cheeseburger machine and, from behind Ricardo's back, shook his head at me, amused by the braggadocio of the reply.

I wanted to hear more. Something less simplistic,

less superficial. And I said, "Well, yes, but lots of men are charming. What do you think was the secret of your particular success with women?"

"My dick is very big," he said earnestly. "I've got a ten-inch dick."

So much for my husband's question, I thought. And so much for the banal Ricardo. I wanted to be done with him. Finished with his boasts, his self-pity, his lies. And unlike all the other women who had eventually come to this view after first taking an interest in him, I could just walk away. I had, finally, just as I'd hoped back when I'd first decided to write about him, exorcised him. There was just one last thing I wanted to ask him, though I knew my chances of getting an honest answer were nil.

"Did you kill Jacqui Bernard?" I said.

"Jacqui?" Ricardo scrunched up his forehead, concentrating. "Jacqui Bernard? Name doesn't ring a bell."

"An older woman. Tall. Very attractive. Lived in Manhattan. On the Upper West Side."

"No." Ricardo shook his head. "I never knew the woman."

EPILOGUE

Ricardo was sent to Attica. I never saw him again. Neither did his wife, Susana. She not only didn't come up from Mexico to visit him, but even ceased responding to his letters. Only Alberto remained in touch, continuing to mail Ricardo packages and to speak with him on the phone from time to time.

"How's he doing?" I asked Alberto one day after he'd had a call from Ricardo.

"Great. There's an element of peace about him now that I never heard in him before. Like, he told me he's begun sleeping the whole night through, something he never did during all those years he was on the run."

"How do you account for it? Is he on medication?"

"No, none at all. I think it's because he's comforted by the structure of prison and the fact that he knows that now there's no chance he'll ever be able to do the kinds of horrible things he did in the past."

Alberto also reported to me on how Ricardo was spending his days. "He's busy all the time. He works in a shop, repairing TV sets. He's taking university courses—studying psychology, anthropology, the law. And he's writing a book."

"About himself?"

"Not exactly. It's fiction, he says, with a character sort of based on himself. He's so into it that it's almost all he ever wants to talk about."

"And you? How do you feel about him now?"

"I feel good about him. I feel that prison is the right place for him—not just because of what he did, but because finally he's not just suffering."

Alberto himself, after all the years he had spent worrying about and trying to come to terms with his brother, seemed finally to be at peace, and I was happy for him.

I was happy, too, for Ed Brown and Janie Becker, who also seemed to be experiencing a kind of peace now that Ricardo was in prison. And I was pleased for Inspector Sanders, my favorite of all the many detectives I'd come to know during my research, for he was promoted to assistant chief of San Francisco's police force.

As to Ricardo's pending cases, nothing further happened. Mexico didn't ask to extradite him to try him for the murder of Laura Gomez, who had attended Mexico City's National University. San Francisco didn't bring him out West to stand trial in the murder of Barbara Taylor, who had been employed in the educational films division of McGraw-Hill. And Los Angeles didn't indict him for the murder of Devon Green, who had worked side by side with him at Scandia. I suppose that the law enforcement authorities in the various locations in which those women had been killed felt it made no sense either economically or administratively to pursue their cases—the pursuit would have been costly and they had plenty of other unresolved murder cases with which to occupy themselves. Why bother with Ricardo when he had already been sentenced to jail for a minimum of thirty-three and a third years and would be close to eighty years old if and when he emerged.

Similarly, New York didn't charge Ricardo with the Manhattan murder of Jacqui Bernard. Indeed, "we've eliminated him in this case," Detective Giorgio, who was in charge of the investigation, informed me the last time I spoke with him.

"How come?" I asked.

"Because Bobby Hines, the detective who was tracking Caputo's movements, established that he wasn't in New York but living in L.A. at the time Bernard was killed."

I was deep into the writing of this book at the time and hated to interrupt my work to do further research. But I was curious about Giorgio's remarks and I immediately called Detective Hines to find out if he'd definitively placed Ricardo in L.A. at the time of Jacqui's murder.

"No," he told me. "That's incorrect. I never did establish where Caputo was at the time Jacqui Bernard was murdered. We don't have a clue as to his whereabouts in the summer of 1983."

"So he could have been in New York?"

"Sure. Personally, I think he was. And personally I wouldn't be surprised if he was responsible not just for the Bernard killing but for a lot of other killings in this country."

So there that was. I put down the phone and went back to writing.

Some months later, I was summering out on the eastern end of Long Island, and one evening I ran into Jacqui Bernard's sister, Henriette, at the home of a mutual friend. Henriette had been the person who'd hired Gordon McEwan all those many years ago, and I'd talked to her from time to time over those years but never in any concentrated way. This time, however, I told her that since the last occasion on which we'd spoken, I'd learned quite a bit about Ricardo Caputo, and she invited me to come visit her and tell her some of what I'd discovered.

The next Sunday I drove to her house, a weatherworn, sprawling place set on a verdant lawn edged with an abundance of purple and white and orange blossoms. Henriette, whose gray hair, dignified air, and smile that swelled her cheeks and crinkled the corners of her eyes reminded me a lot of Jacqui, had been tending those blossoms. A trowel in her hand, she led me to the back of the house, where we sat on a tranquil terrace facing a shimmering pond.

It felt odd to be relating my sorry tale amid such prettiness, but I launched into it, giving Henriette details not just about Natalie Brown, Judith Becker, Barbara Taylor, and Laura Gomez, women with whose sad fates she was already familiar, but about women of whom she'd been unaware, about the mysteriously murdered Devon Green and the painfully traumatized Mary O'Neill, Maria Lopez, and Lotte Angstrom. I told Henriette, too, about my trip to Argentina and my jailhouse interviews with Ricardo, and finally about detectives Giorgio and Hines.

When I was done, Henriette said, "So what do you think? Could Ricardo have killed Jacqui?"

"Yes."

Henriette stared out toward her pond. "I just don't know. I guess that if Jacqui had met Ricardo, she'd have been intrigued by him. She was fascinated by all things Latin American. And I guess that if she'd met him, she'd have been sympathetic to his tales of hardship and wanted to help him out."

"That's what Gordon said," I reminded her.

"Yes, but on the other hand, Jacqui never mentioned to us that she knew anyone of Ricardo's description."

"Was she in the habit of telling you about her men friends?"

"No," Henriette allowed. "She didn't talk much about her personal life. In the ten years before she died, I think she mentioned a man only once or twice."

"Well, you know what they say—you never really know about other people's private lives."

"Not even when the people are members of your own family," Henriette sighed.

"Maybe especially not then."

After that we sat there for a long time, talking about Jacqui and how unique she'd been and reminiscing about how in her final days she'd been all wrapped up in the imminent birth of a grandchild, so excited about it that she'd gotten her daughter-in-law to promise she could be present at the birth.

"She never made it, of course," Henriette said. "My grandniece was born four weeks after we found her body."

"So sad."

"Yes, and so long ago. My grandniece is a teenager now. You know, it's all so long ago that sometimes I can't even remember all the things I felt at the time."

By then it was growing late and the shadows of the trees had begun to lengthen across the green lawn. I had friends coming for dinner that night, I remembered, and told Henriette I had to go.

"Of course," she said, nodding, and began walking me toward my car. As we strolled, she returned to her earlier theme. "Time does have a way of dulling the sharpness of memory."

"I guess that's a blessing."

"I guess." And then, just as I was about to say good-bye and get into my car, Henriette said, "Still, what gets me is that we may never know for sure who killed Jacqui."

"You mean, be absolutely and a hundred percent certain?"

"Yes."

I started to nod my head, and then I realized I didn't agree with her. To my mind, the killer was Ricardo, it had to have been Ricardo. Admittedly, Jacqui had been older than the women Ricardo had confessed to killing, the ones with whom he was known to have been romantically involved. And admittedly her murder had been less brutal than that of those women. But Inspector Sanders had had information that revealed Ricardo to have committed other crimes besides murder, among them armed robbery. And Sanders and so many of the other detectives I had spoken to believed that Ricardo had killed people whose murders he hadn't acknowledged, and possibly that included men as well as women, as Gordon McEwan's informant had asserted, and possibly people who weren't young and people who'd been killed more efficiently than brutally—killed, like Jacqui, during a robbery.

Moreover, when it came to Jacqui, so much pointed in Ricardo's direction. There was the fact that Gordon's informant had said that Ricardo had boasted of having killed her—an unusual thing, surely, to boast about a murder, but a habit of Ricardo's that had been confirmed for me by Guillermo Villanueva in Argentina. There was that friend of Jacqui's who'd told me years ago about Jacqui's having taken up with a younger black or Latin American man she'd met in a bar on Manhattan's Upper West Side, and the bartender at one such establishment who remembered having seen Jacqui and Ricardo come into his place together. There was the super of her building, who had recalled Ricardo's trying to gain access to Jacqui's apartment shortly after she'd been killed, and the fact that although Ricardo claimed to have been in L.A. at the time, this alibi hadn't been verified. But above all, for me, there was the way Ricardo had acted on my visits to him in prison, his coldness, his denials, his lies. I knew none of this was evidence, certainly not the kind of evidence that stands up in courts of law. Yet somehow, for me, the question of who had killed Jacqui no longer felt like a mystery.

"I think we do know," I said softly.

Henriette gazed at me, and I gazed back, and for a moment I saw not Henriette's face but that of her sister. She was smiling at me, her eyes crinkling and her cheeks filling up like the cheeks of the western wind on some ancient map. I murmured good-bye. Not so much to Henriette but to Jacqui. And then I drove home through the gathering dusk.